mirror
work

ALSO BY LOUISE HAY

BOOKS/KIT

FOR CHILDREN

The Adventures of Lulu (with Dan Olmos)
I Think, I Am! (with Kristina Tracy)
Lulu and the Ant: A Message of Love
Lulu and the Dark: Conquering Fears
Lulu and Willy the Duck: Learning Mirror Work

CD PROGRAMS

All Is Well (audio book)
Anger Releasing
Cancer
Change and Transition
Dissolving Barriers
Embracing Change
The Empowering Women Gift Collection
Feeling Fine Affirmations
Forgiveness/Loving the Inner Child
How to Love Yourself
Meditations for Loving Yourself to Great Health (with Ahlea Khadro and Heather Dane)
Meditations for Personal Healing
Meditations to Heal Your Life (audio book)
Morning and Evening Meditations
101 Power Thoughts
Overcoming Fears
The Power Is Within You (audio book)
The Power of Your Spoken Word
Receiving Prosperity
Self-Esteem Affirmations (subliminal)
Self Healing
Stress-Free (subliminal)
The Totality of Possibilities
What I Believe and Deep Relaxation
You Can Heal Your Life (audio book)
You Can Heal Your Life Study Course
Your Thoughts Create Your Life

DVDs

Receiving Prosperity
You Can Heal Your Life Study Course
You Can Heal Your Life, The Movie (also available in an expanded edition)
You Can Trust Your Life (with Cheryl Richardson)

CARD DECKS

Healthy Body Cards
I Can Do It® Cards
I Can Do It® Cards . . . for Creativity, Forgiveness, Health, Job Success, Wealth, Romance
Life Loves You Cards (with Robert Holden)
Power Thought Cards
Power Thoughts for Teens
Power Thought Sticky Cards
Wisdom Cards

CALENDAR

I Can Do It® Calendar (for each individual year)

and

THE ESSENTIAL LOUISE HAY COLLECTION

(comprising *You Can Heal Your Life, Heal Your Body,* and *The Power Is Within You* in a single volume)

All of the above are available at your local bookstore, or may be ordered by visiting:

Hay House USA: **www.hayhouse.com®**
Hay House Australia: **www.hayhouse.com.au**
Hay House UK: **www.hayhouse.co.uk**
Hay House India: **www.hayhouse.co.in**

Louise's websites: **www.LouiseHay.com®**
and **www.HealYourLife.com®**

mirror work

21 DAYS TO HEAL YOUR LIFE

Louise Hay

HAY HOUSE, INC.
Carlsbad, California • New York City
London • Sydney • New Delhi

Published in the United States by: Hay House, Inc.: www.hayhouse
.com® • *Published in Australia by:* Hay House Australia Pty. Ltd.:
www.hayhouse.com.au • *Published in the United Kingdom by:* Hay
House UK, Ltd.: www.hayhouse.co.uk • *Published in India by:*
Hay House Publishers India: www.hayhouse.co.in

Cover design: Nick Charles Welch • *Interior design:* Pamela Homan

Library of Congress Cataloging-in-Publication Data

Names: Hay, Louise L., author.
Title: Mirror work : 21 days to heal your life / Louise Hay.
Description: 1st Edition. | Carlsbad : Hay House, Inc., 2016.
Identifiers: LCCN 2015038471 | ISBN 9781401949822 (paperback)
Subjects: LCSH: Self-acceptance. | Self-esteem. | Self-actualization
  (Psychology) | BISAC: SELF-HELP / Personal Growth / Self-Esteem.
Classification: LCC BF575.S37 .H397 2016 | DDC 158--dc23 LC re-
cord available at http://lccn.loc.gov/2015038471

Tradepaper ISBN: 978-1-4019-4982-2

25 24 23 22 21 20
1st edition, March 2016

Printed in the United States of America

*To all those who are ready to
experience the joy of Mirror Magic.*

CONTENTS

WEEK THREE

WELCOME

Welcome, dear ones, to my 21-day course on mirror work. It is based on my popular video course *Loving Yourself.* Over the next three weeks you will learn how to transform your life simply by looking into a mirror.

Mirror work—looking deeply into your eyes and repeating affirmations—is the most effective method I've found for learning to love yourself and see the world as a safe and loving place. I have been teaching people how to do mirror work for as long as I have been teaching affirmations. Put simply, whatever we say or think is an affirmation. All of your self-talk, the dialogue in your head, is a stream of affirmations. These affirmations are messages to your subconscious that establish habitual ways of thinking and behaving. Positive affirmations plant healing thoughts and ideas that support you in developing self-confidence and self-esteem, and creating peace of mind and inner joy.

The most powerful affirmations are those you say out loud when you are in front of your mirror. The mirror reflects back to you the feelings you have about yourself. It makes you immediately aware of where you are resisting and where you are open and flowing. It clearly shows you what thoughts you will need to change if you want to have a joyous, fulfilling life.

As you learn to do mirror work, you will become much more aware of the words you say and the things you do. You will learn to take care of yourself on a deeper level than you have done before. When something good happens in your life, you can go to the mirror and say, *"Thank you, thank you. That's terrific! Thank you for doing this."* If something bad happens to you, you can go to the mirror and say, *"Okay, I love you. This thing that just happened will pass, but I love you, and that's forever."*

For most of us, sitting in front of a mirror and facing ourselves is difficult at first, so we call this process mirror *work*. But as you continue, you become less self-critical, and the work turns into mirror *play*. Very soon your mirror becomes your companion, a dear friend instead of an enemy.

Doing mirror work is one of the most loving gifts you can give yourself. It takes only a second to say, *"Hi, kid,"* or *"Looking good,"* or *"Isn't this fun?"* It's *so* important to give yourself little positive messages throughout the day. The more you use mirrors for complimenting yourself, approving of yourself, and supporting yourself during difficult times, the deeper and more enjoyable your relationship with yourself will become.

You may be wondering, why 21 days for the program? Can you totally transform your life in just three weeks? Maybe not totally, but you can plant the seeds. As you continue to do your mirror work, these seeds develop into new, healthy habits of mind that open the door to a joyous and fulfilling life.

So let's begin.

HOW TO DOWNLOAD THE DAILY MEDITATIONS

For each of the 21 days of the Mirror Work program, there is a guided meditation. To access the audio meditations, visit www.hayhouse.com/download and enter Product ID: 1516 and Download Code: ebook. If you have any problem accessing the meditation audio, please contact Hay House Customer Care by phone—US (800) 654-5126 or INTL CC+ (760) 431-7695—or visit www.hayhouse.com/contact.

WEEK ONE

Loving Yourself

It's so important to love yourself. Mirror work can help you build the most important relationship of your life: your relationship with yourself.

When you begin your mirror work, you may think it's too easy or even silly. A lot of things I suggest that you do over the next 21 days may at first appear too simple to make a difference. But I have learned that the simplest actions are often the most important. One small change in your thinking can lead to huge changes in your life.

Each day we will address a different theme. I will begin with some thoughts on the theme and then give you a Mirror Work Exercise I would like you to practice throughout the day. You can begin in the morning by doing this exercise in front of your bathroom mirror, and then during the day you can repeat it whenever you pass a mirror or see your reflection in a window.

You can also carry a pocket mirror with you and use it to do mirror work whenever you have a few minutes to spare.

I urge you to keep a journal as you do your mirror work. Jot down your thoughts and feelings so you can see how you are progressing. Each day I will give you a Journaling Exercise, suggesting a few questions to help you get started. I believe that each of us has a power within us, a higher self connected to the Universal Power that loves and sustains us and brings us prosperity of every kind. Journaling will help you connect with this force. You will see that you have within you all that you need to grow and change.

Each day I will also provide you with a Heart Thought to support your mirror work and an affirmation to help you put the day's theme into action. Finally, I offer a guided meditation. I suggest that you sit quietly before you go to bed and reflect on how these ideas can make your life a little easier and a lot better. You can read the meditation in the book or, if you prefer, listen to the audio version from which it was adapted.

Your Day 1 Mirror Work Exercise

1. Stand or sit in front of your bathroom mirror.

2. Look into your eyes.

3. Take a deep breath and say this affirmation: *I want to like you. I want to really learn to love you. Let's go for it and really have some fun.*

4. Take another deep breath and say, *I'm learning to really like you. I'm learning to really love you.*

5. This is the first exercise, and I know it can be a little challenging, but please stay with it. Keep taking deep breaths. Look into your eyes. Use your own name as you say, *I'm willing to learn to love you, [Name]. I'm willing to learn to love you.*

6. Throughout the day, each time you pass a mirror or see your reflection, please repeat these affirmations, even if you have to do it silently.

At first when you do your mirror work, you may feel silly or stupid repeating the affirmations. You may even be angry or want to cry. That's all right—in fact, it's quite normal. And you're not alone. Remember that I'm right here with you. I've been through this, too. And tomorrow is a new day.

The Power Is Within You: Your Day 1 Journaling Exercise

1. After you finish your morning mirror work, write down your feelings and observations. Did you feel angry or upset or silly?

2. Six hours after finishing your morning mirror work, again write down your feelings and observations. As you continued to practice your mirror work formally and informally, did you start to believe what you were saying to yourself?

3. Keep track of any changes in your behavior or your beliefs over the course of the day. Did the exercise get easier, or did you continue to find it difficult after doing it awhile?

4.   At the end of the day, before you go to
     bed, write down what you learned from
     doing your mirror work.

Your Heart Thought for Day 1:
I Am Open and Receptive

If we do mirror work to create good in our lives
but there's a part of us that doesn't believe we are
worth it, we are not going to believe the words we are
saying as we look in the mirror. We will reach a point
at which we start thinking, *Mirror work doesn't work.*

The truth is, the perception that mirror work
doesn't work has nothing to do with the mirror work
itself or the affirmations we say. The problem is that
we don't believe we deserve all the good that life has
to offer.

If that's your belief, then affirm: *I am open and
receptive.*

Your Day 1 Meditation: Loving Yourself
(Day 1 of the audio download)

Each one of us has the ability to love ourselves
more. Each one of us deserves to be loved. We deserve
to live well, to be healthy, to be loved and loving,

and to prosper. And that little child within each of us deserves to grow up into a wonderful adult.

So see yourself surrounded by love. See yourself happy and healthy and whole. And see your life as you would like it to be, putting in all the details. Know that you deserve it.

And then take the love from your heart and let it begin to flow, filling your body and then moving out from you. Visualize the people you love sitting on either side of you. Let the love flow to those on your left and send them comforting thoughts. Surround them with love and support, and wish them well. And then let the love from your heart flow to the people on your right. Surround them with healing energies and love and peace and light. Let your love flow around the room until you are sitting in an enormous circle of love. Feel the love circulating as it goes out from you and then comes back to you multiplied.

Love is the most powerful healing force there is. You can take this love out into the world and silently share it with everyone you meet. Love yourself. Love one another. Love the planet and know that we are all one. And so it is.

DAY 2

Making Your Mirror Your Friend

Today you begin to practice basic mirror work exercises, learning to look closely at yourself and beyond your old beliefs.

It is only the second day of mirror work, and you are just beginning to learn to love and adore yourself. Hang in there. Each day that you practice this new way of thinking about yourself and about life will help erase the old, negative messages you have been carrying for so long. Soon you will be smiling more and finding it easier to look in the mirror. Soon the affirmations will start to feel true.

Now I would like you to take out a pocket mirror or go to your bathroom mirror. Just relax and breathe. Look at yourself in the mirror. Then, using your name, say, *[Name], I love you. I really, really love you.*

Let's say it again, two more times: *I love you. I really, really love you. I LOVE you. I really, really LOVE YOU.*

How does that feel? You can be honest and say that it feels strange or stupid. Because it *does* feel strange and stupid at first. Or maybe you find it hard to do. It's okay to feel this way. Loving yourself unconditionally is something you haven't done before. Let yourself feel these feelings. Whatever you're feeling, it's a beginning, a very good place to start.

I know that telling yourself *I love you* is difficult for many of you. I also know that you can do it, and I'm very proud of you for hanging in. Mirror work will get easier, I promise.

Still, if you find it too hard to say *I love you*, you can start with something a little easier. Maybe try: *I am willing to learn to like you. I am learning to love you.*

When you look in your mirror, I'd like you to imagine that you are talking to a child in kindergarten. Picture yourself as that young kindergartner. Now, using your name, tell this inner child, *[Name], I love you. I really, really love you.*

The more you practice your mirror work, the easier it will get. But remember that it is going to take time. That's why I'd like you to get into the habit of doing your mirror work frequently. Do it when you first get up in the morning. Carry a pocket mirror wherever you go, so you can take it out often and say a loving affirmation to yourself.

Let's affirm: *I am beautiful. I am amazing. I am easy to love.*

Your Day 2 Mirror Work Exercise

1. Stand in front of your bathroom mirror.

2. Look into your eyes.

3. Using your name, say this affirmation: *[Name], I love you. I really, really love you.*

4. Take a few moments now to say it two or three more times: *I really, really love you, [Name].*

5. Keep repeating this affirmation over and over. I want you to be able to say it at least 100 times a day. Yes, that's right: 100 times a day. I know that seems like a lot, but honestly, 100 times a day is easy once you get into the swing of it.

6. So each time you pass a mirror or see your reflection just repeat this affirmation: *[Name], I love you. I really, really love you.*

When you find it difficult to tell yourself *I love you*, it is most likely because you are judging yourself, repeating those old, negative messages. Don't add to your discomfort by judging yourself for making judgments. Just relax and commit to saying the affirmation. Remember: you are committing to an affirmation that's true. The truth is, we *do* love ourselves, when we are not judging ourselves.

It's a good idea to have a tissue at hand when you are doing mirror work, because this work can be very evocative. Often it brings up emotions from the deep. The fact is, we may have been very unkind to ourselves. So when we start to love ourselves again, we become aware of the unloving attitudes we've been carrying for a long time, and that causes a certain amount of grief. But the grief is being released. So let yourself feel what you feel and accept those feelings. Don't judge them. Mirror work is all about self-love and self-acceptance.

I've encouraged you to practice your mirror work first thing in the morning. Sometimes that's the hardest time of day to do it because we feel that we don't look our best in the morning. But that is just a judgment, and what we are doing in mirror work is looking into the mirror without judgment so we can see who we really are.

The Power Is Within You:
Your Day 2 Journaling Exercise

Life is very simple. What we give out, we get back. In your journal, write down your responses to the following questions:

1. What do you want that you are not getting?

2. When you were growing up, what were the rules about deserving? Did you always have to earn in order to deserve? Were things taken away from you when you did something wrong?

3. Do you feel that you deserve to live? To have joy? If not, why not?

As you answer these questions, notice the emotions you are feeling. Write them down in your journal.

Your Heart Thought for Day 2: *I Am Deserving*

Sometimes we refuse to put any effort into creating a good life for ourselves because we believe that we don't deserve it. The belief that we don't deserve it may come from our early-childhood experiences. We might be buying into someone else's concept or opinion that has nothing to do with our own reality.

Deserving has nothing to do with being good. It is our unwillingness to receive the good in life that gets in the way. Allow yourself to accept the good, whether you think you deserve it or not.

Your Day 2 Meditation: A Circle of Love
(Day 2 of the audio download)

See yourself standing in a very safe space. Release your burdens and pain and fear. Release old, negative patterns and addictions. See them falling away from you. Then see yourself standing in your safe place with your arms wide open, saying, *I am open and receptive—* willing to declare for yourself what you want, not what you don't want. See yourself whole and healthy and at peace. See yourself filled with love.

And in this space, feel your connection with other people in the world. Let the love in you go from heart to heart. And as your love goes out, know that it comes back to you multiplied. Send comforting thoughts to everyone and know that these comforting thoughts are returning to you.

On this planet, we can be in a circle of hate, or we can be in a circle of love and healing. I choose to be in a circle of love. I realize that we all want the same things: to be peaceful and safe, and to express ourselves creatively in ways that are fulfilling.

See the world becoming an incredible circle of love. And so it is.

DAY 3

Monitoring Your Self-Talk

Today you learn more about changing the messages you give yourself, clearing out negative thoughts from the past so you can live in the present moment.

Now that you're on Day 3 of your mirror work, are you feeling a closer bond with your friend, your mirror? Each day that you practice mirror work you may fall in love with yourself a little bit more. Each day it becomes easier to say your positive affirmations and truly believe them.

The best way to love yourself is to release all the negative messages from your past and live in the present moment. So today, I'd like to work with you on changing what I call your *self-talk*—what you say to yourself in your head.

Too often we accept the early messages from our parents, our teachers, and other authority figures. You were probably told things like "Stop crying like a baby," "You never clean your room," and "Why won't you make your bed?" And you did what people told you to do, in order to be loved. When you were young, you might have gotten the idea that you were acceptable only if you did certain things. Acceptance and love were conditional. However, it bears remembering that others' approval was based on *their* ideas of what was worthwhile and had nothing to do with your self-worth.

These early messages contribute to our self-talk. The way we talk to ourselves inwardly is really important because it becomes the basis of our spoken words. It sets up the mental atmosphere in which we operate and attracts our experiences to us. If we belittle ourselves, life is going to mean very little to us. However, if we love and appreciate ourselves, then life can be a wonderful, joyous gift.

If your life is unhappy or you are feeling unfulfilled, it is very easy to blame your parents—or the almighty *Them*—and say it is all *their* fault. However, if you do that, you will stay stuck in your conditions, your problems, and your frustrations. Words of blame will not bring you freedom.

Your words have great power. So start listening closely to what you say. If you hear yourself using negative or limiting words, you can change them. If I hear a negative story, I don't go around repeating it to everyone. I think that it has gone far enough, and I let it pass. However, if I hear a positive story, I tell everyone!

When you are out with other people, really listen to what they are saying and how they are saying it. See if you can connect what they say with what they are experiencing in their lives. Many, many people live their lives in *shoulds. Should* is a word that my ear is very attuned to. It is as if a bell goes off every time I hear it. I have heard people say it as many as a dozen times in a single paragraph. These same people wonder why their lives are so rigid, or why they can't leave a situation. They want to have a lot of control over things they cannot control. They are busy either making someone else wrong or making themselves wrong.

You can practice positive self-talk during your mirror work, making only positive statements about yourself and repeating only positive affirmations. If any of the negative self-talk from your childhood comes up, you can turn it around into a positive statement. For example, "You never do anything right!" could become the affirmation *I am a capable person, and I can handle anything that comes my way.* As you listen to yourself and others, you can become more aware of what you say and how and why you say it. This awareness will help you change your self-talk into affirmations that will nurture and heal you in body and mind. What a wonderful way to love yourself!

Let's affirm: *I release all the negative messages from the past. I live in the present moment.*

Your Day 3 Mirror Work Exercise

1. Stand or sit in front of your bathroom mirror.

2. Look into your eyes.

3. Say this affirmation: *Whatever I say to myself, I will say it with love.*

4. Keep repeating it: *Whatever I say to myself in this mirror, I will say it with love.*

5. Is there a statement that you heard as a child that still sticks in your head? Maybe something like "You're stupid" or "You're not good enough," or whatever else comes to mind. Take time to work with negative statements and turn them

into positive affirmations: *I am smart. I am more intelligent than I realize. I am a genius with an abundance of creative ideas. I am a magnificent person. I am lovable. I am worth loving.*

6. Choose one or two of these new, positive affirmations and say them over and over again. Keep saying them until you feel comfortable with them.

7. Each time you pass a mirror or see your reflection in a window throughout the day, stop and repeat these loving affirmations.

The Power Is Within You: Your Day 3 Journaling Exercise

1. Did you repeat a negative story today? Write down how many times you repeated it and how many people you told it to. Now write down something positive you can tell those people tomorrow that will help them feel better about themselves and everyone around them.

2. Write down the word *should*. Next to it, make a list of words to use instead. You might start with the word *could*.

3. Post several of the new, positive affirmations you learned today on your mirror so you can practice them whenever you see them.

Your Heart Thought for Day 3: *I Always Have a Choice*

Most of us have foolish ideas about who we are and many rigid rules about how life should be lived. Let's remove the word *should* from our vocabulary forever. *Should* is a word that makes prisoners of us. Every time we use *should,* we are making ourselves wrong or someone else wrong. We are, in effect, saying: *not good enough.*

What can be dropped now from your *should* list? Replace the word *should* with the word *could.* *Could* lets you know that you have a choice, and choice is freedom. We need to be aware that everything we do in life is done by choice. There is really nothing we *have* to do. We always have a choice.

Your Day 3 Meditation: You Deserve Love
(Day 3 of the audio download)

See yourself surrounded by love. See yourself happy and healthy and whole. See your life as you would like it to be, putting in all the details. Know that you deserve it. Then take the love from your heart and let it begin to flow, filling your body with healing energies. Let your love flow around the room and around your home until you are in an enormous circle of love. Feel the love circulating so that as it goes out from you, it returns to you.

Love is the most powerful healing force there is. Let it wash through your body. You *are* love. And so it is.

Letting Go of Your Past

*Today you start to let go,
release blame, forgive, and move on.*

How did you do yesterday? Do you feel that you are learning to let go of some of your past hurts and tune your self-talk to a more positive channel? I am so proud of you for loving yourself enough to do these lessons every day and to use your mirror work to reprogram all the old tapes you have been playing in your head.

Ever since we were little children, every message we have received, everything we have said, everything we have done, everything we have experienced has been recorded and stored in the filing cabinet in our core, our gut, our solar plexus. I like to imagine that there are little messengers in there and that all our thoughts and experiences are recorded on tapes that the messengers put in the appropriate files.

Many of us have been accumulating files with labels like *I'm not good enough. I'll never make it. I don't do anything right.* We are buried under piles of old, negative tapes.

Today we're going to surprise the little messengers. We're going to do our mirror work and send new messages to our core: *I am willing to let go. I release blame. I am ready to forgive.* The messengers will pick up these new messages and say, "What's this? Where does this get filed? We've never seen this one before."

Can you imagine how wonderful it would be if every day you learned a new way to let go of the past and create harmony in your life? My dear ones, you have already started by doing your daily mirror work. Each day you are clearing out the layers, the blocks of the past. Each time you say an affirmation in front of the mirror, you are removing another layer. What are the layers of your past that are keeping you from living a happy and fulfilling life? What are the blocks preventing you from forgiving yourself and your past?

I think we have trouble identifying these blocks because we honestly don't know what we want to let go of. We know what is not working in our life and we know what we want to have in our life, yet we don't know what's holding us back.

Everything in your life is a mirror of who you are. Just as a mirror reflects your image, your experiences reflect your inner beliefs. You can literally look at your experiences and determine what your beliefs are. If you look at the people in your life, you will see that they are all mirroring some belief you have about yourself. If you are always being criticized at work, it is probably because you are critical and have become the parent who criticized you as a child.

Remember: When something that's happening in your life does not feel comfortable for you, you have the opportunity to look inside and ask, *How am I contributing to this experience? What is it within me that believes I deserve this? How can I change this belief? How can I forgive myself and my past and learn to let go and move on?*

Let's affirm: *I let go of old limitations and beliefs. I let go, and I am at peace.*

Your Day 4 Mirror Work Exercise

1. Stand in front of your bathroom mirror.

2. Take a deep breath and, as you exhale, allow all the tension to leave your body.

3. Look at your forehead and imagine that you are pressing a button that ejects a disk of all the old beliefs and negative thoughts that have been playing in your head. Reach up and imagine that you are pulling this recording out of your head and throwing it away.

4. Now look deeply into your eyes and tell yourself, *Let's make a new recording of positive beliefs and affirmations.*

5. Say these affirmations aloud: *I am willing to let go. I release. I let go. I release all tension. I release all fear. I release all anger. I release all guilt. I release all sadness. I let go of old limitations and beliefs. I let go, and I am at peace. I am at peace with myself. I am at peace with the process of life. I am safe.*

6. Repeat these affirmations two or three times.

7. Throughout the day, whenever any
    difficult thoughts arise, take out
    your pocket mirror and repeat these
    affirmations. Become familiar with them
    so that repeating them becomes a part of
    your daily routine.

The Power Is Within You:
Your Day 4 Journaling Exercise

1. I find that most of the problems in
    our lives are caused by what I call the
    Big Four: Criticism, Fear, Guilt, and
    Resentment. In your journal, create four
    columns, heading each with one of the
    Big Four categories. Think about what role
    they play in your life. Write your thoughts
    and feelings about each category in the
    appropriate column.

2. From Step 1, take the two categories you
    wrote the most about and write down ten
    positive affirmations in each category.
    For example, if one of the categories is
    Resentment, you might write affirmations
    like *I now choose to release all hurt and*

resentment. The more resentment I release, the more love I have to give.

3. Everything in our lives is a mirror of who we are. Think of the people in your life who are the most challenging for you. What are the traits that bother you most about them? Write those down.

4. Look at the traits that you listed in Step 3. Write down how each of these traits mirrors a belief that you have about yourself. You might also want to jot down what you have learned about yourself in doing today's exercises.

Your Heart Thought for Day 4: *I Can Let Go*

We create habits and patterns because they serve us in some way. It is amazing how many illnesses we create because we want to punish a parent. We may not be doing this consciously—in fact, in most cases it is not conscious. But when we start looking within, we find the pattern. We often create negativity because we do not know how to handle some area of life. If that's the case, ask yourself: *What am I feeling sorry about? Who am I angry at? What am I trying to avoid? How do I think this will this save me?*

If you are not ready to let something go—you really want to hold on to it because it serves you—it doesn't matter what you do; you will not be able to let it go. However, when you are ready to let something go, it is amazing how easy it is to release it.

Your Day 4 Meditation: A New Decade
(Day 4 of the audio download)

See a new door opening to a decade of great healing—healing that we have not understood in the past. We are in the process of learning about all the incredible abilities that we have within ourselves. And we are learning to get in touch with those parts of ourselves that have the answers and are there to lead us and guide us in ways that are for our highest good.

See this new door opening wide and imagine stepping through it to find healing in many, many different forms, for healing means different things to different people. Some of us have bodies that need healing; some of us have hearts that need healing; some of us have minds that need healing. So we are open and receptive to the healing that each person needs. We open the door wide for personal growth, and we move through this doorway knowing we are safe. And so it is.

DAY 5

Building Your Self-Esteem

Today you learn more about loving yourself with respect, gratitude, and the realization that your body, mind, and soul are miracles to be appreciated.

How did you feel when you woke up this morning? Did you smile when you looked in the mirror and said, *I love you, darling, I really love you*? Are you starting to believe it? After just a few days of mirror work, you may see that it has already started making a difference in your life. You may be smiling a little more today. You may be feeling much better when you look in the mirror and see your beautiful face. You may be feeling much better about yourself. Are you beginning to love and approve of the person you see in the mirror?

Love is the great miracle cure. Loving ourselves works miracles in our lives. I have discovered that no matter what the problem is, the best way to resolve it is to start loving yourself.

Loving yourself means having great respect for everything about you, inside and out. It is deep gratitude for the miracle of your body and your mind and your soul. Loving yourself is appreciation to such a degree that it fills your heart until it bursts, overflowing with the joy of being *YOU*.

It is impossible to really love yourself unless you have self-approval and self-acceptance. Do you scold and criticize yourself endlessly? Do you believe you are unlovable? Do you live in chaos and disorder? Do you attract lovers and mates who belittle you? Do you mistreat your body with unhealthy food choices and stressful thoughts?

If you deny your good in any way, it is an act of not loving yourself. I remember a woman I worked with who wore contact lenses. When she did her mirror work, she began to release an old fear from her childhood. In a few days, she complained that her contact lenses were bothering her to the point that she couldn't wear them anymore. When she took them out, she looked around and found that her eyesight was almost perfectly clear. Still, she spent the entire day saying, "I don't believe it. I don't believe it." That was her affirmation. The next day, she was back to wearing her contacts. She wouldn't allow herself to believe she had created perfect eyesight, and her disbelief was confirmed. The Universe gave her exactly what she asked for. This is how powerful our thoughts are.

Think how perfect you were when you were a tiny baby! Babies do not have to do anything to become perfect; they already *are* perfect, and they act as if they know it. They know they are the center of the Universe. They are not afraid to ask for what they want. They freely express their emotions. You know when a baby is angry—in fact, the whole neighborhood knows. You also know when babies are happy—their smiles light up a room. They are full of love.

Tiny babies will die if they do not get love. Once we are older, we learn to live without love—or try to—but babies will not stand for it. Babies love every part of their bodies.

You were like that at one time. We were *all* like that. Then we began to listen to adults around us who had learned to be fearful, and we began to deny our own magnificence.

Today, put all criticism and negative self-talk aside. Let go of your old mind-set—the one that berates you and resists change. Release other people's opinions of you.

Affirm: *I am good enough. I am worth loving.*

Your Day 5 Mirror Work Exercise

1. Stand in front of your bathroom mirror.

2. Look into your eyes.

3. Say this affirmation: *I love and approve of myself.*

4. Keep saying it over and over again: *I love and approve of myself.*

5. Repeat this affirmation at least 100 times a day. Yes, that's right: 100 times. Let *I love and approve of myself* become your mantra.

6. Each time you pass a mirror or see your reflection, repeat this affirmation.

This is an exercise I have given to hundreds and hundreds of people over the years. The results are absolutely phenomenal when people stick with it. Remember: mirror work doesn't work in theory; it only works in practice. If you do it, it really will make a difference.

If any negative thoughts come up—such as *How can I approve of myself when I am fat?*, or *It's silly to think that I can think this way*, or *I am no good*—don't resist them, don't fight them, don't judge them. Let them just be there. Stay focused on what you really want to experience, which is to love and approve of yourself. You can gently let go of other thoughts that intrude and stay focused on *I love myself and approve of myself*.

What we are doing in mirror work is trying to get back to the heart of who we really are. We want to experience who we are when we are not judging ourselves.

The Power Is Within You: Your Day 5 Journaling Exercise

1. Write down some of the ways you don't love yourself or ways you express your lack of self-worth. Do you criticize your body? Do you talk down to yourself?

2. Write down some of the negative opinions you think others have of you. For each of these negative opinions, write down an affirmation to turn it into a positive statement. For example, you could change

My mother thinks I'm fat to *I am beautiful exactly as I am.*

3. Make a list of all the reasons why you love yourself. Make another list of why people love to spend time with you.

4. Post these loving lists where you can see them every day.

Your Heart Thought for Day 5: *I Love Being Me*

Can you imagine how wonderful it would be if you could live your life without ever being criticized by anyone? Wouldn't it be wonderful to feel totally at ease, totally comfortable? You would get up in the morning and know you were going to have a wonderful day, because everybody would love you and nobody would put you down. You would feel just great.

You know what? You can give this to yourself. You can make the experience of living with yourself the most wonderful experience imaginable. You can wake up in the morning and feel the joy of spending another day with *you.*

Your Day 5 Meditation:
Affirmations for Self-Esteem
(Day 5 of the audio download)

I am totally adequate for all situations.

I choose to feel good about myself.

I am worthy of my own love.

I stand on my own two feet.

I accept and use my own power.

It is safe for me to speak up for myself.

I am loved and accepted exactly as I am, right here and right now.

My self-esteem is high because I honor who I am.

My life gets more fabulous every day. I look forward to what each new hour brings.

I am neither too little nor too much, and I do not have to prove myself to anyone.

Life supports me in every possible way.

My consciousness is filled with loving, positive, healthy thoughts that are reflected in my experience.

The greatest gift I can give myself is unconditional love. I love myself exactly as I am. I no longer wait to be perfect in order to love myself.

DAY 6

Releasing
Your Inner Critic

*Today you learn to break the habit of
judgment and self-criticism, and to go
beyond the need to put yourself down.*

Look in your mirror today and take a few moments
to congratulate yourself! You are beginning to love
and approve of yourself—or at least to be willing to
do so. Wherever you are in the process, celebrate the
progress you have made so far. I celebrate *you* and your
commitment to your mirror work.

The more mirror work you do, the more aware of
your self-talk you become. If I asked you to play a tape
of your inner dialogue today, what would it sound
like? Would you be listening to negative affirmations
like *I am so stupid. I'm such a klutz. Nobody asks me what
I think. Why are there so many inconsiderate people?* Is

your inner voice constantly picking, picking, picking at everything? Are you seeing the world through critical eyes? Do you judge everything? Do you stand in self-righteousness?

So many of us have such a strong habit of judgment and criticism that we cannot easily break it. I used to be a constant complainer, full of self-pity. I loved to wallow in the pits. I didn't know that I was perpetuating situations in which to pity myself. I didn't know any better in those days.

It is so important to do your mirror work, because it makes you acutely aware of judgments and negative self-talk and allows you to release your inner critic as soon as you can. You will never be able to love yourself until you go beyond the need to put yourself down and make life wrong.

As a little baby, you were so open to life. You looked at the world with eyes of wonder. Unless something was scary or someone harmed you, you accepted life just as it was. Later, as you grew up, you began to accept the opinions of others and make them your own. You learned how to criticize.

What helped me eventually was that I started to listen to what I was saying. I became aware of my inner critic, and I worked to stop my self-criticism. I began to say positive affirmations in front of my mirror without quite knowing what they meant. I just kept saying them over and over again. I started with the easy ones: *I love myself. I approve of myself.* Then I graduated to these: *My opinions are valued. I release the need to criticize myself. I release the need to criticize others.*

After a while I started noticing that positive changes were beginning to take place. When you work on releasing your inner critic, you, too, will begin to notice changes. I believe that criticism shrivels our spirits. It reinforces the belief *I am not good enough.* It certainly doesn't bring out the best in us. But when you release the inner critic, you get in touch with your higher self.

So let's check: Are you learning to play a tape of positive affirmations in your mind? Are you paying attention to your thoughts and replacing negative thoughts with positive affirmations?

By doing mirror work, you will become more aware of your inner voice and what you say to yourself. Then you'll be able to release the need to pick on yourself all the time. And when you do, you will notice that you no longer criticize others so much.

When you make it okay to be yourself, then you automatically allow others to be themselves. Their little habits no longer bother you as much. You release the need to change others as you want them to be.

Then, as you stop judging others, they release the need to judge you. Everybody gets to be free.

Our feelings are thoughts in action. There is no need to feel any guilt or shame about them. They serve a purpose, and when you release negative thoughts from your mind and body, you allow space inside for other, more positive feelings and experiences.

Let's affirm: *It is now safe for me to release my inner critic and move into love.*

Your Day 6 Mirror Work Exercise

1. Find a quiet place with a mirror where you will feel safe and where you won't be disturbed.

2. Look into the mirror. Look straight into your eyes. If you are still uncomfortable doing this, then concentrate on your mouth or your nose. Talk to your inner child. Your inner child wants to grow and blossom, and needs love, acceptance, and praise.

3. Now say these affirmations: *I love you. I love you, and I know you are doing the best you can. You are perfect just as you are. I approve of you.*

4. You may want to do this exercise several times before you truly feel that your inner voice is less critical. Do what feels right for you.

The Power Is Within You:
Your Day 6 Journaling Exercise

1. Make a list of five things you criticize yourself for.

2. Go down the list, and beside each item write the date on which you began to criticize yourself for this particular thing. If you can't remember the exact date, approximate.

3. Are you amazed at how long you've been picking on yourself? This habit of self-criticism has not produced any positive changes, has it? Criticism doesn't work! It only makes you feel bad. So be willing to stop it.

4. Change each of the five criticisms on your list to a positive affirmation.

5. Carry this list with you. When you notice yourself being judgmental, take out the list of affirmations and read it a few times. Better yet, read it aloud in front of your mirror.

Your Heart Thought for Day 6:
I Love and Accept Myself Exactly as I Am

We all have areas of our lives that we think are unacceptable and unlovable. If we are really angry with parts of ourselves, we often engage in self-abuse. We abuse alcohol, drugs, or cigarettes. We overeat. We beat ourselves up emotionally. One of the worst things we do, which causes more damage than anything else, is criticize ourselves. We need to stop all criticism. Once we get into the habit of not criticizing ourselves, it is amazing how we stop criticizing other people. We realize that everyone is a reflection of us, and what we see in another person we can see in ourselves.

When we complain about someone, we are really complaining about ourselves. When we can truly love and accept who we are, there is nothing to complain about. We cannot hurt ourselves, and we cannot hurt another person. Let's make a vow that we will no longer criticize ourselves for anything.

Your Day 6 Meditation:
We Are Free to Be Ourselves
(Day 6 of the audio download)

In order to be whole, we must accept all of ourselves. So let your heart open, and make plenty of room in there for all parts of yourself: the parts you are proud of, the parts that embarrass you, the parts you reject, and the parts you love. They are all you. You're beautiful. We all are. When your heart is full of love for yourself, then you have so much to share with others.

Let this love now fill your room and radiate out to all the people you know. Mentally put the people you care about in the center of your room, so that they can receive the love from your overflowing heart.

Now see the child in each of these people dancing as children dance, skipping and shouting and turning somersaults and cartwheels, filled with exuberant joy, expressing all the best of the child within. And let your inner child go and play with the other children. Let your child dance. Let your child feel safe and free. Let your child be all that it ever wanted to be.

You are perfect, whole, and complete, and all is well in your wonderful world. And so it is.

DAY 7

Loving Yourself: A Review of Your First Week

Today you look at how far you've come and how much you've accomplished toward breaking free of your old beliefs and discovering future possibilities.

Congratulations, dear ones! You have made it through your first week of mirror work. I am so proud of you for sticking with this course and practicing your mirror work these past seven days.

Mirror work takes time, and I am so glad you have given yourself these 21 days to learn it. The more you practice, the easier it will get. It's okay if you still feel a bit silly or uncomfortable when you look in your mirror. Saying *I love you, I really love you* to ourselves is hard for most of us at first. It may take several weeks or even a month to be entirely comfortable saying these loving words to yourself. But once you can say them with more ease, you will see positive changes in your life.

Over the past seven days, you have invited your mirror to become your friend and constant companion. You have learned how it will help you become much more aware of what you say and do. You have taken time to listen to your self-talk and to practice your positive affirmations.

Again, I want to emphasize that doing mirror work is a true act of love, one of the most loving gifts you can give yourself. Each day that you practice your mirror work, you may fall in love with yourself a little bit more. The best way to love yourself is to release all the junk from your past—the self-judgments, the old stories that hold you back—so you can live in the present moment. We have all gotten into the habit of believing negative statements we have heard since childhood. When you can turn these negative affirmations into positive statements and practice them looking into your mirror, you can let go of some of these past hurts and move on.

Each day that you do your mirror work, you are clearing out the layers of the past. Each time you say an affirmation in the mirror, you are removing another block in these layers. It has taken years for these layers to form, built of blocks like the bricks that make up a large wall. It will take time to break through these layers, but you can start with one block. Each time you remove one block or one layer, you allow more light and love to shine through. As you begin to believe the positive affirmations you say in your mirror, more of this beautiful love will break through the walls of your past. No matter what the problem is, the best way to resolve it is by loving yourself.

If every now and then you hear the voice of your inner critic picking on you for something or making a negative remark, it is okay. You always have your friend and companion—your mirror—to turn to. Look yourself deeply in the eyes and say, *I am worth loving.* And keep up the good work!

Let's affirm: *I celebrate this week of loving myself with mirror work. I now move into a new space of consciousness in which I am willing to see myself differently.*

Your Day 7 Mirror Work Exercise

1. Stand in front of your bathroom mirror.

2. Look into your eyes.

3. Say these affirmations: *I love you. I really love you. And I'm so proud of you for doing your mirror work.*

4. Repeat these affirmations ten times, adding your name: *I love you, [Name]. I really love you. I love you, [Name]. I really love you. And I'm so proud of you for doing your mirror work.*

5. Look at your forehead and imagine that you are pressing a button there and ejecting a disk of your old beliefs and negative thoughts that has been playing in your head. Take your hand and imagine that you are pulling that disk out of your head and throwing it away.

6. Now look deeply in your eyes and imagine that you are making a new CD of positive affirmations: *I am willing to let go. I am worth loving. I am perfect just the way I am.*

The Power Is Within You: Your Day 7 Journaling Exercise

1. Take out your journal and open it to the first exercise you did, on Day 1.

2. Read the feelings and observations you wrote down after your mirror work on Day 1.

3. On a new page, write down your feelings and observations after the first week of doing your mirror work. Are the exercises getting easier? Are you feeling more comfortable looking in the mirror?

4. Write down where you are having the most success with your mirror work. Write down where you are having the most difficulty.

5. Create new affirmations to help you in those areas where you are having blocks.

Your Heart Thought for Day 7:
All My Experiences Are Right for Me

We have been going through doors since the moment we were born. That was a big door and a big change, and we have been through many doors since then.

We came to this lifetime equipped with everything we need in order to live fully and richly. We have all the wisdom and knowledge we need. We have all the abilities and talents we need. We have all the love we need. Life is here to support us and take care of us. We need to know and trust that this is so.

Doors are constantly closing and opening, and if we stay centered in ourselves, then we will always be safe, no matter which doorway we pass through. Even when we pass through the last doorway on this planet, it is not the end. It is simply the beginning of another new adventure. Trust that it is all right to experience change.

Today is a new day. We will have many wonderful new experiences. We are loved. We are safe.

Your Day 7 Meditation: Spirit Am I
(Day 7 of the audio download)

We are the only ones who can save the world. As we band together for the common cause, we find the answers. We must always remember that there is a part of us that is far more than our bodies, far more than our personalities, far more than our dis-eases, and far more than our past. There is a part of us that is more than our relationships. The very core of us is pure Spirit, eternal. It always has been and always will be. We are here to love ourselves and to love one another. By doing this, we will find the answers so that we can heal ourselves and the planet.

We are going through extraordinary times. All sorts of things are changing. We may not even know the depth of the problems, yet we are swimming as best we can. This, too, shall pass, and we will find solutions. We connect on a spiritual level, and on the level of Spirit, we are all one. We are free. And so it is.

WEEK TWO

DAY 8

Loving Your Inner Child—Part One

*Today you look beyond the adult you
see in the mirror and meet your inner child.*

This is a very important day in your mirror work. Take my hand, and let's walk over to your mirror. Look deeply into your eyes. Look beyond the adult you see in your mirror and greet your inner child.

It doesn't matter how old you are; there is a little child within you who needs love and acceptance. If you are a woman, no matter how self-reliant you are, you have a little girl inside who is very tender and needs help. If you are a man, no matter how self-confident you are, you have a little boy inside of you who craves warmth and affection.

When you look in the mirror, do you see your inner child? Is this child happy? What is this child trying to tell you?

Every age you have been is within you—in your consciousness and your memory. As a child, when something went wrong, you tended to believe that there was something wrong with *you*. Children develop the idea that if only they could do everything right, then their parents would love them and wouldn't punish them.

Often we turn off or tune out around the age of five. We make that decision because we think there is something wrong with us, and we're not going to have anything to do with this child anymore.

There is a parent inside of us as well. And for most of us, this inner parent is scolding the inner child almost nonstop. If you listen to your inner dialogue, you can hear the scolding. You can hear the parent tell you what you are doing wrong or that you are not good enough.

So way back in childhood we began a war with ourselves and started criticizing ourselves the way our parents criticized us: *You're stupid. You're not good enough. You don't do anything right.* This constant criticism became a habit. Now, as adults, most of us either totally ignore the child within us or belittle the child in the same way we were belittled in the past. We repeat this pattern over and over.

Every time you feel scared, realize that it is the child within you who is scared. The adult isn't afraid, yet it has disconnected and isn't there for the child. The adult and the child need to develop a relationship with each other.

How do you connect with your inner child? The first step is getting to know the child through your mirror work. Who is this child? Why is this child unhappy? What can you do to help this child feel safe and secure and loved?

Talk to your inner child about everything you do. I know it may sound silly, but it works. Let your inner child know that no matter what happens, you will never turn away from it or leave it but will always be there for it and love it.

All your inner child really wants is to be noticed, to feel safe, and to be loved. If you can take just a few moments a day to begin to connect with the little person inside of you, life is going to be a lot better.

Let's affirm: *I am willing to love and accept my inner child.*

Your Day 8 Mirror Work Exercise

1. Find a photo of yourself when you were about five years old. Tape the photo to your bathroom mirror.

2. Look at the photo for a few minutes. What do you see? Do you see a happy child? A miserable child?

3. Talk to your inner child in the mirror. You can look at the photo or even look into your own eyes—whichever feels more comfortable for you. If you had a nickname as a child, use this name as you speak to your inner child. What works really well is to sit in front of the mirror, because if you are standing, as soon as difficult feelings start to come up, you might be tempted to run out the door. So sit down, grab a box of tissues, and start talking.

4. Open your heart and share your innermost thoughts.

5. When you are finished, say these affirmations: *I love you, dear one. I am here for you. You are safe.*

The Power Is Within You:
Your Day 8 Journaling Exercise

1. For this exercise, you will need crayons, colored pencils, or colored felt-tip pens.

2. Using your nondominant hand—the one you don't write with—draw a picture of yourself as a child. Be creative!

3. Tape the drawing to your bathroom mirror.

4. Look at the picture and begin talking to your inner child.

5. Ask your child the following questions and write down the answers in your journal: *What do you like? What do you dislike? What frightens you? What do you need? What can I do to make you happy?*

6. Close your eyes and take a few minutes to reflect on what you've learned about your inner child.

Your Heart Thought for Day 8:
I Embrace My Inner Child with Love

Take care of your inner child. It is the child who is frightened. It is the child who is hurting. It is the child who does not know what to do.

Be there for your child. Embrace it and love it and do whatever you can to take care of its needs. Be sure to let your child know that no matter what happens, you will always be there for it. You will never turn away or desert it. You will always love this child.

Your Day 8 Meditation:
Let Go and Relax
(Day 8 of the audio download)

Take a nice, deep breath and close your eyes. Take another deep breath and allow your body to completely relax. Let your attention move to your toes and allow them to go completely limp. Now relax your insteps, your heels, and your ankles. Let your feet become heavy. Allow this relaxation to move up your calves and into your knees. Continue to move this warmth and relaxation into your thighs, feeling them become heavier.

Now let your hips and your buttocks relax. Allow your waistline to release and then feel the peacefulness move up into your chest, expanding through your collarbone and into your shoulders. Allow your upper arms to let go. Let your elbows relax. Let your lower arms, wrists, and hands relax. Let the last of the tension move out through your fingertips. Let your neck relax, and then your jaw, your cheeks, and all the muscles around your eyes. Let your forehead and scalp relax. Let go, let go, let go. Relax.

DAY 9

Loving Your Inner Child—Part Two

Today you use mirror work to forgive the past and begin to love the beautiful child within.

How are you and your inner child doing today? Are you getting to know each other a little better? I have found that working with the inner child is extremely valuable in helping to heal the hurts of the past. We are not always in touch with the feelings of the frightened little child within us.

If your childhood was full of fear and physical or verbal battles, you may have a habit of mentally beating yourself up. When you do this, you are continuing to treat your inner child in much the same way. The child inside, however, has no place to go.

Many of us have an inner child who is lost and lonely and feels rejected. Perhaps the only contact we have had with our inner child for a long time is to scold and criticize it. Then we wonder why we are unhappy. We cannot reject a part of ourselves and still be in harmony within.

Today, let's use our mirror work to move beyond our parents' limitations and connect with the little lost child inside. Let's forgive the past and begin to love this beautiful child within. This child needs to know that we care.

Most of us have buried many feelings and hurts from the past. Learning to love your inner child is going to take time. Take all the time you need. Return to these exercises again and again. You will get there, I promise.

Your inner child still carries the beliefs you developed early on. If your parents had rigid ideas and you are now very hard on yourself or you tend to build walls around you, your inner child is probably still following your parents' rules. If you continue to pick on yourself for every mistake, it must be very scary for your inner child to wake up in the morning thinking, *What is my parent going to yell at me about today?*

What our parents did to us in the past was a product of their consciousness. We are the parents now.

We are using our consciousness now. If you are still refusing to take care of your inner child, you are stuck in your own resentment. Invariably that means there is someone you still need to forgive. What resentment do you need to let go of? What haven't you forgiven yourself for?

For now, visualize that you are taking your inner child by the hand and going everywhere together for a few days. See what joyous experiences you can have. This may sound silly, but please try it. It really works. Create a wonderful life for yourself and your inner child. The Universe will respond, and you will find ways to heal your inner child and the adult you.

No matter what your early childhood was like— happy or sad—you and only you are in charge of your life now. You can spend your time blaming your parents, or you can embrace love.

Love is the biggest eraser I know. It erases even the deepest and most painful memories, because love goes deeper than anything else. Think for a moment: Do you want a life of pain or one of joy? The choice and power are always within you. Look into your eyes, and love yourself and the little child within.

Let's affirm: *I love my inner child. I am in charge of my life now.*

Your Day 9 Mirror Work Exercise

1. Go to your bathroom mirror and look at the picture of yourself as a child that you taped to it yesterday.

2. Take a moment right now and tell your inner child that you care. Say these affirmations: *I care about you. I love you. I really love you.*

3. Sit in front of your mirror, if you can, or sit and look into a handheld mirror. Continue the conversation with your inner child that you began yesterday. You could open with an apology, saying something like *I'm sorry I haven't talked to you over the years. I'm sorry I scolded you for so long. I want to make up for all the time we spent apart from each other.*

4. If you haven't talked to your inner child in 50 or 60 years, it may take some time before you feel like you're reconnecting. But be persistent. Eventually you will make a connection. You may *feel* the child inside you. You may *hear* the child inside you. You may even *see* the child inside you.

5. Keep your tissue box nearby. It's okay to cry while you are talking to your inner child. Tears will help you to break through and connect with the child inside you.

The Power Is Within You: Your Day 9 Journaling Exercise

1. When you were little, what did you really like to do? Write down everything that comes to mind. When was the last time you did any of these things? Too often, the parent inside us will stop us from having fun because it's not the adult thing to do.

2. Now put down your journal and go outside and play with your little child. Have fun! Do the silly things you loved to do when you were young, like jumping in a pile of leaves or running under the garden sprinkler. Watch other children at play. It will bring back memories of the games you enjoyed. If you want more fun in your life, make the connection with

your inner child and come from that
space of spontaneity. I promise that you
will start having more fun.

Your Heart Thought for Day 9:
I Am Willing to Change and Grow

You are willing to learn new things because you do
not know it all. You are willing to drop old concepts
when they no longer work for you. You are willing to
see your behavior and say, "I don't want to do that anymore." You know you can become more of who you
are. Not become a better person—that would imply
that you are not good enough, which isn't true—but
more of who you *really* are.

Growing and changing is exciting, even if you
have to look at some painful things within yourself in
order to do so.

Your Day 9 Meditation:
Loving the Inner Child
(Day 9 of the audio download)

Go back in time. See yourself as a little child of
five. Hold out your arms to this child and say, "I am
your future, and I have come to love you." Embrace

this child lovingly, and then bring it with you to the present time. See the two of you standing at a mirror, looking at each other lovingly. And as you stand there, become aware that there are so many parts of you that are missing.

Now go back in time even further, to the very moment you were born. You've just come down the birth canal. It may have been a difficult trip. You feel the cold air and see the bright lights, and someone may have just smacked you. You have arrived! You are here to live a whole lifetime. Love that little tiny baby. Love that baby!

Now move forward in time to the moment when you began to walk. You would stand up and fall down, stand up and fall down, and stand up and fall down. And then suddenly you were standing, and you took a step and another step, and you were walking! You were so proud of yourself. Love that little child. Love that child!

Then move forward in time to your first day at school. You didn't want to leave your mother, but you did. You took your first steps over the threshold of your school. You were scared, but you did it. You were doing the very best you could. Love that child. Love that child!

Then remember your life around the age of ten and everything that was going on then. It may have been wonderful; it may have been difficult. You were doing the very best you could to survive, and you made it. Love that child. Just love that child!

Now go forward to the time you were entering puberty and remember all that was going on. It was exciting and scary and maybe more than you could handle, but you got through it. You did the best you could, and you made it. So love that teenager. Love that teenager!

Go to the time of your first job and how exciting it was to earn money. You wanted so badly to make a good impression, and there was so much to learn. But you did the best you could and you succeeded. Love that person. Just love that person!

Remember the first time you were rejected in love and how much your heart hurt. You were sure no one would ever love you again. You were in such pain. You did the best you could, and you made it. Love that person. Love that person!

Then go to another milestone in your life. It might have been embarrassing or painful or wonderful. Whatever it was, you were doing the best you could at that time, with the understanding, knowledge, and awareness that you had then. So love that person. Love that person!

Now gather all the many parts of yourself and bring them forward to the present. See yourself standing in front of the mirror with all of your selves and realize that you are looking at the richness and fullness of your life. Of course, there were difficult times and painful times and embarrassing times and times of confusion. And that's all right. That's all part of life. Love *all* of yourself.

Now turn around. And as you look ahead, see a person standing before you with arms outstretched, saying, "I am your future, and I have come to love you."

Life is an endless opportunity to love yourself—past, present, and future. Loving and accepting every part of yourself is healing. How can you possibly be whole or healed if you are rejecting any part of yourself? Healing is to make yourself whole again. Love yourself, every part of yourself, and be whole. All is well. And so it is.

Loving Your Body, Healing Your Pain

The lesson today is about pain:
what it is, where it comes from, what it's
telling you, and what you can learn from it.

Many of us live with pain or illness on a daily basis. It may be a small part of our lives, or it may take up a large portion of it. Today you are going to use your mirror work to open a new door to loving your body and healing your pain.

No one wants to be in pain, but if you have it, what can you learn from it? Where does pain come from? What is it trying to tell you? Since pain can be a manifestation of either physical or mental dis-ease, it is clear that both the body and mind are susceptible to it.

I recently witnessed a wonderful example of this as I watched two little girls playing in a park. The first child raised her hand to playfully slap her friend on the arm. Before she was able to make contact, the other little girl cried, "Ow!" The first girl looked at her friend and asked, "Why did you say, 'Ow'? I haven't even touched you yet." Her friend replied, "Well, I knew it was gonna hurt."

The body, like everything else in life, is a mirror of our inner thoughts and beliefs. It is always talking to us, if we will only take the time to listen. I believe we create every pain and illness in our body. Every cell within our body responds to every single thought we think and every word we speak.

The body is always aspiring to achieve optimum health, no matter what we do. However, if we abuse the body with unhealthy food and unhealthy thoughts, we contribute to our discomfort.

Pain comes to us in many forms: an ache, a scratch, a stubbed toe, a bruise, congestion, uneasy sleep, a queasy feeling in the stomach, a dis-ease. It is trying to tell us something. Pain is the body's way of waving a red flag to get our attention—a last-ditch effort to inform us that something is wrong in our life.

When we feel pain, what do we do? We usually run to the medicine cabinet or the drugstore and take a pill. When we do this, we are saying to our body, "Shut up! I don't want to hear you." Your body will quiet down for a while, but then the whispering will return—this time a little louder than before. Imagine what would happen if you were telling your friend something important but she wasn't listening. You would say it again, probably louder. If she still didn't listen, you might well become agitated and lash out. Or, feeling hurt and unloved, you might shut down.

Sometimes people actually *want* to be sick. In our society, we've made pain and illness a legitimate way to avoid responsibility or unpleasant situations. If we cannot learn to say no, then we may have to invent a dis-ease to say no for us.

At some point, however, you have to pay attention to what's going on. Allow yourself to listen to your body, because fundamentally your body wants to be healthy, and it needs you to cooperate with it.

Think of every pain you have as a teacher, telling you that there's a false idea in your consciousness. Something you are believing, saying, doing, or thinking is not for your highest good. I always picture the body tugging at me, saying, "*Please* pay attention!" When you discover the mental pattern behind a pain or illness, you have a chance to change the pattern through your mirror work and arrest the dis-ease.

Are you willing to pay attention to your body and release the need that has contributed to your pain? If so, get started on your mirror work and learn to love your body and heal your pain.

Let's affirm: *I love my body. I return my body to optimal health by giving it what it needs on every level.*

Your Day 10 Mirror Work Exercise

1. Choose the pain or illness you would like to work on today. Let's say it's heartburn.

2. Stand or sit in front of your mirror.

3. Look deeply into your eyes, and ask yourself these questions: *Where did this heartburn come from? What is it trying to tell me? Have I been eating unhealthy foods? Is there something that I am fearful about? Did I hear some news that I'm not able to digest? Is there a heated situation that I'm not dealing with? What or who can't I stomach?*

4. Regardless of what pain or dis-ease you are experiencing, you can say these affirmations: *I breathe freely and fully. I*

listen to the messages of my body. I feed my body healthy and nourishing food. I allow my body to rest when needed. I love my amazing body. I am safe. I trust the process of life. I am fearless. Keep repeating the affirmations.

5.   Now do some affirmations specifically for the area causing you pain. (You can look up mental patterns for pain and particular illnesses, along with corresponding affirmations, in my book *Heal Your Body.)* If you're having stomach problems, for example, you can say: *I love my stomach. I really love you, my healthy stomach. I feed you healthy foods, and you digest them with joy. I give you permission to be well.*

6.   Repeat these affirmations two or three more times.

The Power Is Within You: Your Day 10 Journaling Exercise

1.   When you feel pain or discomfort, take time to quiet yourself. Trust that your Higher Power will let you know what

needs to be changed in your life so you can be free of this pain.

2. Visualize a perfect natural setting with your favorite flowers growing in abundance all around you. Feel and smell the sweet, warm air as it blows gently across your face. Concentrate on relaxing every muscle in your body.

3. Ask yourself these questions: *How am I contributing to this problem? What is it that I need to know? What areas of my life are in need of change?* Meditate on these questions and let the answers arise. Write down the answers in your journal.

4. Choose one of the answers you received in Step 3 and write an action plan that you can work on today.

Make changes one step at a time. As the Chinese philosopher Lao-tzu said, "The journey of a thousand miles begins with a single step." One small step added to another can create significant change in your life. Pain does not necessarily disappear overnight, though it may. It has taken time for pain to surface; therefore it may take some time to recognize that it is no longer needed. Be gentle with yourself.

Your Heart Thought for Day 10:
I Listen Carefully to My Body's Messages

The body, like everything else in life, is a mirror of your inner thoughts and beliefs. Every cell responds to every single thought you think and every word you speak.

In this world of change, you choose to be flexible in all areas. You are willing to change yourself and your beliefs to improve the quality of your life and your world. Your body loves you in spite of how you may treat it. Your body communicates with you, and you now listen to its messages. You are willing to get the message.

You pay attention and make the necessary corrections. You love your body and give it what it needs on every level to bring it back to optimal health. You call upon an inner strength that is yours whenever you need it.

Your Day 10 Meditation:
Positive Affirmations for Health
(Day 10 of the audio download)

Here are some positive affirmations to support your health and healing. Repeat them often:

I enjoy the foods that are best for my body.

I love every cell of my body.

I make healthy choices.

I have respect for myself.

I look forward to a healthy old age because I take loving care of my body now.

I am constantly discovering new ways to improve my health.

I return my body to optimum health by giving it what it needs on every level.

Healing happens. I get my mind out of the way and allow the intelligence of my body to do its healing work naturally.

I have a special guardian angel. I am divinely guided and protected at all times.

Perfect health is my divine right, and I claim it now.

I am grateful for my healthy body. I love life.

I am the only person who has control over my eating habits. I can always resist something if I choose to.

Water is my favorite beverage. I drink lots of water to cleanse my body and mind.

Filling my mind with pleasant thoughts is the quickest road to health.

DAY 11

Feeling Good,
Releasing Your Anger

*Today you address anger: how to process it
and release it before it makes you sick, and how to
allow space inside for more positive emotions.*

How does it feel to be talking to yourself every
day and telling yourself that you are loved? Look in
your mirror and take a few moments to congratulate
yourself. You have looked deep into your emotions
and started to release the past. You are now learning
to play a positive tape of affirmations in your mind.
Celebrate the progress you have made so far. I celebrate
YOU and your commitment to your mirror work.

While you were digging into your past and releasing your emotions, you may have discovered some
angry feelings aimed at yourself or a particular event.
So today I'd like to help you work on forgiving and

releasing any anger you might have, so that you can feel good about yourself.

Anger is an honest emotion. But when it is not expressed or processed outwardly, it will be processed inwardly, in the body, and usually develops into a disease or dysfunction of some sort.

We generally get angry about the same things over and over again. When we are angry, we feel we don't have a right to express it, so we swallow it, which can cause resentment, bitterness, or depression. So it's good to handle our anger and release it whenever it comes up.

If you feel like expressing yourself physically, then get some pillows and start hitting them. Don't be afraid to let your anger take its natural course. You have already kept your feelings bottled up too long. There is no need to feel any guilt or shame about feeling angry.

One of the best ways to deal with anger is to talk openly to the person you are angry with. When you feel like screaming at someone, then the anger has been building up for a long time. Often it is because you feel you cannot speak openly to the other person. So the second-best way to let our anger out is to talk to the person in the mirror.

Mirror work will help you get all your feelings out. One of my students had a difficult time letting her anger out. Intellectually, she understood her feelings, yet she couldn't express them outwardly. When she allowed herself this expression through her mirror work, she was able to scream and call her mother and her alcoholic daughter all sorts of names. She felt a tremendous weight lift from her when she released her resentment. Later, when her daughter came to visit, the woman couldn't stop hugging her. All this was possible because she had released her repressed anger, making room for love.

So many people tell me how much happier they are once they release anger toward another person. It is as though a huge burden has been lifted.

Go within and know that there is an answer to your anger and that you will find it. It is very healing to meditate and visualize the rage flowing freely out of your body. Send love to the person who is the object of your anger and see your love dissolve whatever disharmony there is between you. Be willing to become harmonious. Perhaps the anger you feel is reminding you that you are not communicating well with others. By recognizing this, you can correct it.

Let's affirm: *It is okay to have my feelings. Today I express how I am feeling in positive ways.*

Your Day 11 Mirror Work Exercise

1. Find a place with a mirror where you will feel safe and will not be disturbed.

2. Look into your eyes in the mirror. If you are still uncomfortable doing this, then concentrate on your mouth or nose.

3. See yourself and/or the person you believe has wronged you. Remember the moment when you became angry and let yourself feel the anger come through you. Begin to tell this person exactly what you are so angry about. Express all the anger you feel. Be specific. You could say something like: *I am angry at you because [fill in the reason]. I am hurt because you [fill in the reason]. I am so afraid because you [fill in the reason].*

4. You may need to do this exercise several times before you truly feel that you have gotten rid of all your anger. You may want to work on one anger issue or several. Do what feels right for you.

The Power Is Within You:
Your Day 11 Journaling Exercise

1. Have you been angry for much of your life? Here are some questions you can journal about to help release these habitual angry feelings: *Why am I choosing to be angry all the time? What am I doing to create situation after situation that angers me? Who am I still punishing? What am I giving out that attracts in others the need to irritate me?*

2. Now ask yourself these questions and write down your answers: *What do I want? What makes me happy? What can I do to make myself happy?*

3. Think about ways you can create a new space inside you to feel good about yourself. Think about ways you can create optimistic and cheerful patterns and beliefs.

Your Heart Thought for Day 11:
I Deserve to Feel Good

Life is very simple. We create our experiences by our patterns of thought and feeling. What we believe about ourselves and about life becomes true for us. Thoughts are only words strung together. They have no meaning whatsoever. It is *we* who give meaning to them. We give meaning to them by focusing on the negative messages over and over in our minds.

What we do with our feelings is very important. Are we going to act them out? Will we punish others? Sadness, loneliness, guilt, anger, and fear are all normal emotions. But when these feelings take over and become predominant, life can be an emotional battlefield.

Through mirror work, self-love, and positive affirmations, you can nourish yourself and relieve any of the anxiety you may be feeling at the moment. Do you believe you deserve peace and serenity in your emotional life?

Let's affirm: *I release the pattern in my consciousness that is creating resistance to my good. I deserve to feel good.*

Your Day 11 Meditation: Your Healing Light
(Day 11 of the audio download)

Look deep within the center of your heart and find a tiny pinpoint of brilliantly colored light. It is such a beautiful color. It is the very center of your love and healing energy. Watch the little pinpoint of light begin to pulsate. As it pulsates, it expands until it fills your heart. See this light moving through your body to the top of your head and the tips of your toes and fingers. You are absolutely glowing with this beautiful colored light, with your love and your healing energy. Let your whole body vibrate with this light. Say to yourself: *With every breath I take, I am getting healthier and healthier.*

Feel this light cleansing your body of dis-ease and allowing vibrant health to return to it. Then let this light begin to radiate out from you in all directions, so that your healing energy touches everyone who needs it. What a privilege it is to share your love and light and healing energy with those who are in need of healing. Let your light move into hospitals and nursing homes and orphanages, and into prisons, mental hospitals, and other institutions of despair, bringing hope and enlightenment and peace. Let it move into every home in the city in which you live. Wherever there is pain and suffering, let your love and light and healing energy bring comfort to those in need.

Select one place on the planet as a place you would like to help heal. It may be far away or just around the corner. Concentrate your love and light and healing energy on this place and see it come into balance and harmony. See it whole. Take a moment every day to send your love and light and healing energy to the particular place you have chosen.

What we give out comes back to us multiplied. Give your love. And so it is.

DAY 12

Overcoming Your Fear

*Today you learn about how to
defuse the power fear has over you
and trust that life is taking care of you.*

Look in your mirror, take a deep breath, and blow a kiss to that beautiful person who is looking back at you. You are getting stronger each day. Thank your mirror for helping you release your past and reflect more positive thoughts your way. Life loves you, and so do I!

Today your mirror work is on an emotion that can block you from loving yourself, forgiving others, and having the happy life you deserve. This emotion is fear.

Fear is rampant on the planet today, in the form of war, murder, greed, and mistrust. Fear is a lack of trust in yourself. When you can overcome your fear, you will begin to trust life. You will begin to trust that life is taking care of you.

In her international bestseller *Feel the Fear . . . and Do It Anyway*, Susan Jeffers wrote, "If everybody feels fear when approaching something totally new in life, yet so many are out there 'doing it' despite the fear, then we must conclude that *fear is not the problem*." She believed that the real issue is not the fear itself but how we *hold* it. We can approach fear from a position of power or from a position of helplessness. The fact that we have the fear becomes irrelevant.

How much power do you give to your fears?

When a fearful thought comes up, it is really just trying to protect you. When you become physically frightened, adrenaline pumps through your body to protect you from danger, and the same thing happens with the fear you manufacture in your mind.

I suggest that when you do your mirror work, you talk to your fear. You can say, "I know you want to protect me. I appreciate that you want to help me. And I thank you." Acknowledge the fearful thought for wanting to take care of you.

By observing your fears and addressing them during your mirror work, you will begin to recognize that you are *not* your fears. Think of your fears the way you view images on a movie screen: what you see on the screen is not really there. The moving pictures are just frames of celluloid that go by in a flash. Your fears will come and go just as rapidly, unless you insist on holding on to them.

Fear is only a limitation of your mind. You fear getting sick or becoming jobless or losing a loved one or having your partner leave you. Then fear becomes a defense mechanism. It would be much more powerful, however, to do your mirror work so that you can stop re-creating fearful situations in your mind.

I believe that we have a choice between love and fear. We experience fear of change, fear of not changing, fear of the future, and fear of taking a chance. We fear intimacy, and we fear being alone. We fear letting people know what we need and who we are, and we fear letting go of the past. But the mind cannot hold two opposing thoughts at once, and at the other end of the spectrum from fear is love. Love is the miracle worker we're all looking for. When you love yourself, you can take care of yourself.

When you are frightened, remind yourself that it means you are not loving and trusting yourself. The belief that you are not good enough is often at the root of your fears. But when you love and approve of yourself *completely*, you can begin to overcome your fears.

Do everything you can to strengthen your heart, your body, and your mind. Turn to your mirror and the power within you.

Let's affirm: *All is well. Everything is working out for my highest good. I am safe. Love is my strength. Only love is real.*

Your Day 12 Mirror Work Exercise

1. What is the greatest fear you are experiencing now? Write it on a Post-it® note and stick the note on the left side of your mirror. Acknowledge this fear. Tell it: *I know you want to protect me. I appreciate that you want to help me. I thank you. Now I let you go. I release you and I am safe.* Then take the sticky note, rip it up, and toss it in the trash or flush it down the toilet. However you get rid of the fear, the point is to release it.

2. Look in the mirror again and repeat these affirmations: *I love and trust. Love and life take care of me. I am one with the Power that created me. I am safe. All is well in my world.*

3. Now look in the mirror and observe your breathing. We often hold our breath when we're frightened. If you are feeling threatened or fearful, consciously breathe. Take a few deep breaths. Breathing opens the space inside you that is your power. It straightens your spine, opens your chest, and gives your tender heart room to expand.

4. Continue breathing naturally and observing your breath. As you do this, repeat these affirmations: *I love you, [Name]. I love you. I really love you. I trust life. Life gives me everything I need. There is nothing to fear. I am safe. All is well.*

The Power Is Within You: Your Journaling Exercise for Day 12

1. Write down your greatest fears under the following headings: *Family, Health, Career, Relationships,* and *Finances.*

2. Then write one or more positive affirmations for each fear you listed. For

example, if you wrote *I'm afraid I'll get sick and won't be able to take care of myself,* then an affirmation might be *I will always attract all the help I need.*

Your Heart Thought for Day 12:
I Am Always Perfectly Protected

Remember: when a fearful thought comes up, it is just trying to protect you. Tell the fear, "I appreciate that you want to help me." Follow that with an affirmation to address that particular fear. Acknowledge and thank the fear, but don't give it power or importance.

Your Day 12 Meditation:
Creating a Safe and Loving World
(Day 12 of the audio download)

Think of today and every day as a time of learning, a new beginning. It is an opportunity to change and grow, to open your consciousness to a new level and consider new ideas and new ways of thinking, to envision the world we dream of living in. Our vision helps to create the world. Come with me as we see ourselves and our planet in new and powerful ways.

Envision a world where everyone has dignity, where everyone, no matter what race or nationality, feels empowered and secure. See children everywhere being treasured and valued as all child abuse disappears. See schools using their precious time to teach children important things like how to love themselves, how to have relationships, how to be parents, how to handle money and be secure financially. Then see all the sick people being made well again, dis-ease becoming a thing of the past as doctors learn to keep people healthy and vital. See pain and suffering disappearing and hospitals being turned into apartment buildings.

Envision all the homeless taken care of and jobs available for everyone who wants to work. See prisons building self-worth and self-esteem in guards and prisoners alike, releasing responsible citizens who love life. See churches removing sin and guilt from their teaching and supporting their members in expressing their divine magnificence and finding their highest good. See governments really caring about the people, with justice and mercy available to all. See honesty and fairness returning to all businesses as greed becomes unknown. See men and women empowering one another to live in dignity as all acts of violence are eliminated. See pure water and nourishing food and clean air being the norm for all of us.

Now let's walk outside and feel the clean rain. And as it stops, clouds fade away and we see a beautiful rainbow as the sun comes out. Notice the clear air. Smell its freshness. See sparkling water in streams and lakes. Notice the lush vegetation: dense forests, abundant flowers, and fruits and vegetables available to everyone.

All over the world, see everyone enjoying peace and plenty, with harmony among all people. As we lay down our arms and open our hearts, see judgment, criticism, and prejudice becoming old-fashioned and fading away. See borders crumbling, separation disappearing. See us all becoming one—truly brothers and sisters who care about one another.

See the planet, our Mother Earth, healed and whole, natural disasters dissipating as the earth breathes a sigh of relief and peace reigns.

Think about other positive things you would like to see happening on this planet. As you continue to hold these ideas in your mind and envision them, you are helping to create this new safe and loving world.

DAY 13

Starting Your Day with Love

Today you discover that how you start your morning can determine your experiences for the day. You learn how the power of positivity can change everything for the better.

Congratulations! You have made it through the first 12 lessons of this course. You have learned how to use the tool of mirror work to change your belief patterns and release unhealthy emotions. Are you beginning to feel the power of mirror work and how it can change your life?

Today you'll learn how to use your mirror work to help heal specific areas of your life. Let's begin with how you start your day. Did you know that the first hour of the morning is crucial? How you spend it will determine your experience of the rest of your day.

mirror work

How did *you* start your day today? When you woke up, what were the first words that came out of your mouth? Did you complain? Did you think about what wasn't working in your life?

How you start your day is often how you live your life.

What do you say when you first look in the bathroom mirror? What do you say when you take a shower? What do you say when you get dressed? How do you leave your house for work? Do you just run out the door, or do you say something nice first? What do you do when you get into the car? Do you slam the door and growl about going to work, or do you bless the traffic on your journey?

Too many people start off their day with "Oh, shit! It's another day and I've got to get up, damn it!" If you have a lousy way of starting your day, you're not going to have a good day—ever. It's not possible. If you do your best to have the morning be awful, your day will be awful.

I have a little routine I've done for years. The moment I wake up, I snuggle my body a little deeper into my bed and thank my bed for a really good night's sleep. I do this for a few minutes as I start my day with positive thoughts. I tell myself things like: *This is a good day. This is going to be a really good day.*

Then I get up, use the bathroom, and thank my body for working well.

I spend a little time stretching, too. I have an exercise bar in the doorway of the bathroom that I can use to stretch my entire body. I hold the bar, bring my knees up to my chest three times, and then hang by my arms. I find that stretching my body in the morning is very good for maintaining flexibility and health.

After I do a few stretches, I make a cup of tea and take it back to bed. I love my bed. I had the headboard specially built at an angle so I can lean up against it when I read or write.

Stretching my body and mind is my morning ritual. Then I start to get up. I try to give myself two hours before I face the rest of the day. I like to be able to do things in a leisurely way. I've learned to take my time.

If you are a busy mom or dad who needs to get the children ready for school, or if you have to get to work early, it's important to give yourself some time to start your day off in the right way. I would rather wake up earlier to have this extra time in the morning. Even if you give yourself only 10 or 15 minutes, this is absolutely essential. It's your time for self-care.

When you get up, it's important to do a ritual that feels good to you and to say something to yourself that makes you feel good. Set in motion the best day possible for yourself. You don't have to make these changes in your life all at once. Just pick one ritual for the morning and start there. Then once you have the ritual down, pick another one and keep practicing. Don't overwhelm yourself. Remember: the idea is to feel good.

Let's affirm: *Today I create a wonderful new day and a wonderful new future.*

Your Day 13 Mirror Work Exercise

1. When you first wake up in the morning and open your eyes, say these affirmations to yourself: *Good morning, bed. Thank you for being so comfortable. I love you. This is a blessed day. All is well. I have time for everything I need to do today.*

2. Now take a few more minutes to relax and let these affirmations flow through your mind, then feel them in your heart and throughout the rest of your body.

3. When you're ready to get up, go to your bathroom mirror. Look deeply into your

eyes. Smile at that beautiful, happy, relaxed person looking back at you!

4. As you're looking in the mirror, say these affirmations: *Good morning, [Name]. I love you. I really, really love you. There are great experiences coming our way today.* And then say something nice to yourself like: *Oh, you look wonderful today. You have the best smile. I wish you a terrific day today.*

The Power Is Within You: Your Day 13 Journaling Exercise

1. Create a morning ritual for yourself. Write down all the steps you can take to start your morning in a positive, happy, and supportive way.

2. Write down two or three affirmations you can say for each of the steps in your morning ritual. Write affirmations for when you get dressed, when you make your breakfast, and when you get in your car and drive to work.

3. If you would like more examples of affirmations for your daily ritual, see the affirmations in the back of *You Can Create an Exceptional Life,* the book I wrote with Cheryl Richardson.

Your Heart Thought for Day 13:
I Open New Doors to Life

You are standing in the corridor of life, and behind you many doors have closed. The doors represent things you no longer do or say or think, experiences you no longer have. Ahead of you is an unending corridor of doors, each one opening to a new experience.

As you move forward, see yourself opening doors on wonderful experiences you would like to have. See yourself opening doors to joy, peace, healing, prosperity, and love. Doors to understanding, compassion, and forgiveness. Doors to freedom. Doors to self-worth and self-esteem. Doors to self-love. It is all here before you. Which door will you open first?

Trust that your inner guide is leading you in the ways that are best for you and that your spiritual growth is continuously expanding. No matter which door opens or which door closes, you are always safe.

Your Day 13 Meditation:
Positive Affirmations for Love
(Day 13 of the audio download)

Allow these affirmations to fill your consciousness, knowing they will become true for you. Practice them often, with joy:

From time to time, I ask those I love how I can love them more.

I choose to see clearly with eyes of love. I love what I see.

I draw love and romance into my life, and I accept it now.

Love is around every corner, and joy fills my entire world.

I rejoice in the love I encounter every day.

I am comfortable looking in the mirror and saying, "I love you. I really, really love you."

I now deserve love, romance, joy, and all the good that life has to offer me.

I am surrounded by love. All is well.

I am in a joyous, intimate relationship with someone who truly loves me.

I am beautiful, and everybody loves me.

I am greeted by love wherever I go.

I attract only healthy relationships. I am always treated well.

I am very thankful for all the love in my life. I find it everywhere.

DAY 14

Loving Yourself: A Review of Your Second Week

Today you review your progress in your mirror work and learn how to give yourself more time and encouragement on the journey.

How proud I am of you, dear ones! Here it is the end of our second week, and there you are in front of your friend, your mirror, practicing and learning each day the many ways you can reflect more love back into your life! You deserve love and joy and all the good that life has to offer you.

You may still feel a little silly or uneasy doing your mirror work. That's okay. I encourage you to be patient with yourself as you embark on new exercises each day. Change can be difficult, or it can be easy. Remember that this is a journey of self-love and acceptance, and acknowledge all the effort you are making.

You have accomplished so much already. You have seen how your mirror helps you become much more aware of what you say and do. You are learning how to let go of whatever does not serve you. You are becoming more aware of your self-talk, listening carefully to your words and learning how to turn them around into positive affirmations. You are also working hard to transform your inner critic into an admiring fan who will praise and compliment your efforts and your commitment to change. Good for you!

Your inner child was the subject of two lessons this past week, and you bravely tackled them both. Give yourself a big cheer! You introduced yourself to your inner child, and you are beginning to understand what this little one is feeling. You are also finding time to hold this child in your arms and let it know how safe and loved it is. I am so proud of you for taking this enormous step toward loving yourself.

After these first 14 lessons, you are discovering how your body mirrors your inner thoughts and beliefs. You are beginning to pay attention to your body's messages. You are beginning to feed your body the loving nourishment it needs: encouraging thoughts and positive affirmations. You are also noticing how good you can feel when you express your true feelings and emotions, even if they are negative ones. You must also congratulate yourself for all the hard work and exercises you are doing to release your anger toward others. This is such a healing experience that can truly change your life.

By observing your fears and addressing them during your mirror work, you have learned another very important lesson this week: *you are not your fears.* Fear is only a limitation of your mind. You always have a choice between love and fear.

You have also been practicing one of my favorite principles this week: *how you start your day is often how you live your life.* It makes me so happy to know you are making an effort to start your day with loving thoughts. This sets a positive tone for the rest of your beautiful day.

See how much you have already learned in just 14 days? Continue to give yourself every encouragement as you go through this new experience of mirror work. Always know that I am here by your side.

Let's affirm: *Here I am, world—open and receptive to all the wonderful things that this mirror-work course is teaching me.*

Your Day 14 Mirror Work Exercise

1. Find a photo of yourself as a child at a time when you were truly happy. Perhaps you have a snapshot taken at your birthday party, or while you were doing something with friends or visiting one of your favorite places.

2. Tape this photo to your bathroom mirror.

3. Talk to that vibrant and happy child in the photo. Tell this child how much you want to feel that way again. Discuss with your inner child your true feelings and what's holding you back.

4. Say these affirmations to yourself: *I am willing to let go of all my fears. I am safe. I love my inner child. I love you. I am happy. I am content. And I am loved.*

5. Repeat these affirmations ten times.

The Power Is Within You:
Your Day 14 Journaling Exercise

1. Take out your journal and open it to the first exercise you did on Day 7.

2. Read the feelings and observations you wrote down when you did your mirror work that day.

3. On a new page, write down your feelings and observations today, after the second week of mirror work. Are the exercises getting easier for you? Are you feeling more comfortable looking in the mirror?

4. Write down where you are having the most success. Write down where you are having the most trouble.

5. Create a new mirror work exercise and affirmations to help you in those areas where you are experiencing blocks.

Your Heart Thought for Day 14:
I Am Willing to See Only My Magnificence

Choose to eliminate from your mind and your life every negative, destructive, fearful idea and thought. No longer listen to or become part of detrimental thoughts or conversations. Today no one can harm you because you refuse to believe in being hurt. You refuse to indulge in damaging emotions, no matter how justified they may seem to be. You rise above anything that attempts to make you angry or afraid. Destructive thoughts have no power over you.

You think and say only what you want to create in your life. You are more than adequate for all you need to do. You are one with the Power that created you. You are safe. All is well in your world.

Your Day 14 Meditation: Feel Your Power
(Day 14 of the audio download)

Welcome this new day with open arms and love. Feel your power. Feel the power of your breath. Feel the power of your voice. Feel the power of your love. Feel the power of your forgiveness. Feel the power of your willingness to change.

You are beautiful. You are a divine, magnificent being. You deserve all good—not just some good, but *all* good. Feel your power and be at peace with it, for you are safe.

WEEK THREE

Forgiving Yourself and Those Who Have Hurt You

Today's lesson is about forgiveness—forgiving yourself and those who have hurt you, thus opening your heart to a new level of loving yourself.

For the past two weeks, you have worked on releasing many of the old beliefs that were blocking you. I know it wasn't an easy task, so give yourself time to celebrate your progress. How does it feel today to look in your mirror and feel so much lighter? Take a deep breath in. Now release this breath and say, "Ahh! I am letting go of my past, and I feel great!"

Forgiveness is a difficult area for all of us. We build up these blocks that bind us for many years. Take my hand, and together let's work on learning to forgive ourselves and those who have hurt us. You can do it.

Forgiveness opens our hearts to self-love. If you have a problem with loving yourself, you can get stuck in an unforgiving state. Many of us carry grudges for years and years. We may feel self-righteous because of what someone did to us. I call this being stuck in the prison of self-righteous resentment. We get to be right, but we never get to be happy.

You may disagree and say, "But you don't know what that person *did* to me. It's unforgivable." Being unwilling to forgive is a terrible thing to do to yourself. Bitterness is like swallowing a teaspoon of poison every day. It accumulates and harms you. It's impossible to be healthy and free when you keep yourself bound to the past.

One of the biggest spiritual lessons you can learn is to understand that everyone is doing the best they can at any given moment. People can do only so much with the understanding, awareness, and knowledge they have. Invariably, people who mistreat others were themselves mistreated in childhood. The greater the level of violence, the greater their inner pain and the more they may lash out. This is not to say that their behavior is acceptable or excusable. However, for your own spiritual growth, you must be aware of their pain.

The incident you are holding on to is over—perhaps long over. Let it go. Allow yourself to be free. Come out of this personal prison you have built and step into the sunshine of life. If the situation is continuing, then ask yourself why you think so little of yourself that you still put up with it. Why do you stay in such a situation?

You have a choice: you can stay stuck and bitter, or you can do yourself a favor by willingly forgiving the past and letting it go, and then moving on to create a joyous, fulfilling life. You have the freedom to make your life anything you want it to be, because you have freedom of choice.

The purpose of today's lesson is to help you raise your self-esteem to such a level that you will allow only loving experiences in your life. Please do not waste your time trying to get even. It will not work. What you give out always comes back to you. So drop the past and work on loving yourself now. Then you can have a wonderful future.

One of the most valuable lessons I have learned is that when you do your forgiveness work, it is not necessary to go to the people involved and tell them that you forgive them. Sometimes you will want to do this, but you do not have to. The major work in forgiveness is done in your own heart and in front of your mirror.

Remember, forgiveness is seldom for others. It is for you.

So many people have told me that they have truly forgiven someone, and then a month or two later they have received a phone call or email from that person, asking to be forgiven. This seems to happen most often after doing forgiveness exercises in front of a mirror. So as you do the mirror work exercises in today's lesson, let yourself experience your feelings deeply.

Let's affirm: *As I forgive myself, it becomes easier to forgive others.*

Your Day 15 Mirror Work Exercise

I believe you receive the most benefit from forgiveness work when you do it in front of a mirror. I suggest finding a mirror you can sit in front of comfortably. I like to use the long mirror on the back of my bedroom door. Give yourself time to do this exercise. And you will probably want to repeat it often. Most of us have a lot of people to forgive.

1. Sit in front of your mirror and close your eyes. Breathe deeply several times. Feel yourself grounded on your chair.

2. Think of the many people who have hurt you in your life. Let them pass through your mind. Now open your eyes and

begin to talk to one of them—aloud. Say something like "You hurt me deeply. I thought I would never get past this. However, I will not stay stuck in the past any longer. I am willing to forgive you." If you can't do that yet, just affirm, *I am willing.* Your willingness is all it takes to move toward forgiveness.

3. Take a breath and then say to the person, "I forgive you. I set you free." Breathe again and say, "You are free. I am free."

4. Notice how you feel. You may feel resistance or you may feel relief. If you feel resistance, just breathe and affirm: *I am willing to release all resistance.*

5. As you continue to do this exercise, today or another day, expand your list of people to forgive. Remember: forgiveness is not an event; it's a process. You may need to keep working on one person a little longer, each time going a little deeper into forgiveness.

This may be a day when you can forgive several people. It may be a day when you can forgive only one. It doesn't matter. However you do this exercise is the right way for you. The universe and forgiveness see your showing up. At times forgiveness is like peeling away the layers of an onion. If there are too many layers, put the onion away for a day or so. You can always come back and peel another layer. Acknowledge yourself for even being willing to do this exercise. You are healing.

The Power Is Within You: Your Day 15 Journaling Exercise

1. Put on some soft music—something that will make you feel relaxed and peaceful. Now take your journal and a pen, and let your mind drift.

2. Go back into the past and think of all the things that you're angry with yourself about. Write them down. Write them *all* down. You may discover that you have never forgiven yourself for the humiliation of wetting your pants in the first grade. What a long time to carry that burden!

3. Now take this list and write a positive affirmation for each item. If you wrote *I'll never forgive myself for [incident]*, then your affirmation could be: *This is a new moment. I am free to let go.* Remember that sometimes it's easier to forgive others than to forgive yourself. Often we demand perfection of ourselves and are harder on ourselves than on others. However, it's time to go beyond this old attitude. Forgive yourself. Let it go. Give yourself the space to be spontaneous and free.

4. And now put down your journal and go outside—to a beach, a park, even an empty lot—and let yourself run. Don't jog; run—wild and free. Do somersaults. Skip along the street and laugh while you're doing it! Take your inner child outdoors with you and have some fun. So what if someone sees you? This is for your freedom!

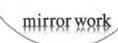

Your Heart Thought for Day 15:
I Can Forgive

I am one with life, and life loves me and supports me. Therefore, I claim for myself an open heart filled with love. We are all doing the best we can at any given moment, and this is also true for me. The past is over and done. I am not my parents or their patterns of resentment. I am my own unique self, and I choose to open my heart and allow love, compassion, and understanding to flush out all memories of past pain. I am free to be all that I can be. This is the truth of my being, and I accept it as so. All is well in my life.

Your Day 15 Meditation: For Forgiveness
(Day 15 of the audio download)

Here are some positive affirmations for forgiveness. Repeat them often.

The door to my heart opens inward. I move through forgiveness to love.
As I change my thoughts, the world around me changes.
The past is over, so it has no power now. The thoughts of this moment create my future.

It is no fun being a victim. I refuse to be helpless anymore. I claim my own power.

I give myself the gift of freedom from the past and move with joy into the now.

There is no problem so big or so small that it cannot be solved with love.

I am ready to be healed, I am willing to forgive, and all is well.

I know that old, negative patterns no longer limit me. I let them go with ease.

As I forgive myself, it becomes easier to forgive others.

I forgive myself for not being perfect. I am living the very best way I know how.

It is now safe for me to release all of my childhood traumas and move into love.

I forgive everyone in my past for all perceived wrongs. I release them with love.

All of the changes in life that lie before me are positive ones, and I am safe.

DAY 16

Healing Your Relationships

*Today you learn about releasing an
old love, healing a broken relationship,
and looking for a new love.*

Forgiveness is the miracle cure we have all been looking for. You probably feel much lighter and more beautiful today. Celebrate your freedom and surround yourself with love.

Indeed, love is our topic for today. You may want to release an old love or heal a broken relationship, or maybe you are looking for a new love. I want you to look in your mirror right now. Do you see that wonderful and loving person looking back at you? This is the most important person you know: yourself!

If you want to heal a relationship, the first relationship you need to improve is the one you have with yourself. Why would anyone want to be with you if *you* don't want to be with you? When you are happy with yourself, then all your other relationships improve, too. A happy person is very attractive to others. If you are looking for more love, then you need to love yourself more. It is as simple as that.

This means no criticism, no complaining, no blaming, no whining, and no choosing to feel lonely. It means being very content with yourself in the present moment and choosing to think thoughts that make you feel good *now*.

There is no one way to experience love, for everyone experiences it in different ways. For some of us to really experience love, we need to *feel* love through being hugged and touched. Others need to *hear* the words *I love you*. Still others need to *see* a demonstration of love, such as a gift of flowers. Often our preferred way of receiving love is the way we feel most comfortable demonstrating it in return.

I suggest that you use your mirror and work on loving yourself continually every day. Say your loving affirmations every moment you can. Demonstrate the growing love you have for yourself. Treat yourself to romance and love. Pamper yourself. Show yourself how special you are. Life always mirrors back to us the feelings we have inside. As you develop your inner sense of love and romance, the right person to share your growing sense of intimacy will be attracted to you like a magnet.

If you want to go from loneliness thinking to fulfillment thinking, then you need to create a loving mental atmosphere within and around you. Let any negative thoughts about love and romance fade away. Instead, think about sharing love, approval, and acceptance with everyone you meet.

When you truly love who you are, you will stay centered, calm, and secure, and your relationships at home and at work will be wonderful. You will find yourself reacting to people and situations differently. Matters that were once desperately important to you will not seem quite as crucial anymore. New people will enter your life, and perhaps some old ones will disappear. This may be scary at first, but it can also be refreshing and exciting.

Remember: when you think joyous thoughts, you will be a happy person. Everyone will want to be with you, and all of your relationships will improve and flourish.

Let's affirm: *Deep in the center of my being is an infinite well of love. I am love.*

Your Day 16 Mirror Work Exercise

1. Go back to your lesson on mirror work from Day 2.

2. Stand in front of your mirror.

3. Look deeply into your eyes and say these affirmations: *I love you. I really love you.*

4. Using your name this time, look deeply into your eyes and say, I *love you, [Name]. I really love you.* These affirmations are worth repeating over and over again.

5. If you are having trouble in your relationships, look into your eyes, breathe deeply, and say, *I am willing to release the need for relationships that don't nourish and support me.* Repeat this five times in the mirror, and each time you say it, give it more meaning. Think of specific relationships as you say it.

The Power Is Within You:
Your Day 16 Journaling Exercise

1. In your journal, write about how you experienced love as a child. Did you observe your parents expressing love and affection? Were you raised with lots of hugs? In your family was love hidden behind fighting, crying, or silence?

2. Write ten affirmations of love and practice them in front of your mirror. Here are some examples: *I am worthy of love. The more I open to love, the safer I am. Today I remember that life loves me. I let love find me at the perfect time.*

3. Write down ten things that you love to do. Pick five and do them today.

4. Take several hours and pamper yourself: buy yourself flowers, treat yourself to a healthy meal, show yourself how special you are.

5. Repeat Step 3 every day this week!

Your Heart Thought for Day 16:
I Live in a Circle of Love

Envelop your family in a circle of love, whether family members are living or not. Broaden the circle to include your friends, your loved ones, your co-workers, everyone from your past, and all the people you would like to forgive but don't know how. Affirm that you have wonderful, harmonious relationships with them all, with respect and caring on both sides.

Know that you can live with dignity and peace and joy. Let this circle of love envelop the entire planet, and let your heart open so that you have space within you for unconditional love.

Your Day 16 Meditation: Love Is Healing
(Day 16 of the audio download)

Love is the most powerful healing force there is. Send everyone you know lots of comfort and acceptance and support and love. Be aware that as you send these thoughts out, you also receive them in return.

Visualize a circle of love that embraces your family members, whether living or not, as well as friends, co-workers, and everyone from your past. Put yourself in the circle. You are worth loving. You are beautiful.

You are powerful. Open yourself to all good and to the unconditional love within you. Affirm:

I open myself to love.

I am willing to love and be loved.

I see myself prospering. I see myself healthy. I see myself creatively fulfilled.

I have wonderful, harmonious relationships in which there is mutual respect and caring.

DAY 17

Living Stress Free

*Stress is a fear reaction to life
and its constant changes. Today you
learn how to stop feeling so stressed.*

From your letters and your comments on my Facebook page, I notice that many of you are struggling with much stress in your lives. Do you know why you feel so stressed?

Stress is a fear reaction to life and to the constant change that is inevitable. *Stress* has become a catchword: we use it as an excuse for not taking responsibility for our feelings, above all our fear. But if you can equate *stress* with *fear*—and understand that feeling stressed is really a fearful reaction—you can begin to eliminate the *need* for stress in your life.

A peaceful, relaxed person is neither frightened nor stressed. So if you're feeling stressed, ask yourself what you are afraid of. Most people have a long list of worries, with things like work, money, family, and health at the top. Your concern then becomes how to eliminate the fear and move through life feeling safe. You can start by doing your mirror work and practicing positive affirmations. When you do this, you can replace your negative, constricting thoughts with positive thoughts that create peace, joy, harmony, and a stress-free life.

There is an expression I like to use a lot: *the totality of possibilities.* I learned it from one of my early teachers in New York. This expression always gave me a taking-off place for letting my mind go beyond what I thought possible—far beyond the limited beliefs I grew up with.

As a child, I did not understand how much of the criticism grown-ups heaped on me was not deserved. It was their reaction to a stressful or disappointing day. But I accepted their criticism as true, and the negative thoughts and beliefs about myself that I internalized were limitations that conditioned my life for many years. I may not have looked awkward or dumb or silly, but I sure felt it.

Most of our beliefs about life and about ourselves are formed by the time we are five years old. We may expand on them a little as teenagers and maybe a tiny bit more when we are older, but very little changes overall. If I were to ask you why you hold a certain belief, you would almost certainly trace it back to a decision you made when you were a young child.

So we live in the limitations of our five-year-old consciousness. These limitations often stop us from experiencing and expressing the totality of possibilities. We think things like *I'm not smart enough. I'm not organized. I have too much on my plate. I don't have enough time.* How many of you are letting limiting beliefs stop you?

You have a choice to accept these limitations or to go beyond them. Remember: the limitations you feel are all in your mind and have nothing to do with reality. When you learn to drop your limiting beliefs and allow yourself to move into the totality of possibilities, you will discover that you *are* good enough. You *do* have what it takes. You *can* handle whatever is on your plate. And you have all the time you need. You can see all sorts of possibilities, and you are capable of remarkable things.

Let's affirm: *I become more confident and proficient every day. There are no limits to my abilities.*

Your Day 17 Mirror Work Exercise

1. For this exercise, I'd like you to start by sitting in a comfortable chair with your hands in your lap and both feet flat on the floor. Now close your eyes and take three long, deep breaths. Breathe in slowly and breathe out. Breathe in and breathe out. Imagine that you are wearing your tension and fear as an overcoat. Imagine undoing the buttons and pulling the coat off your shoulders, sliding it over your arms, and dropping it on the floor. Feel any fear and tension flowing out of your body. Feel your muscles relax. Allow your entire body to relax.

2. Now pick up your pocket mirror and look deeply into your eyes. Say: *I release all fear. I let go of all tension. I am at peace. Freedom from stress is my divine right.* Keep repeating these affirmations over and over again.

3. Close your eyes and take a few more minutes to breathe deeply. Repeat these affirmations: *I believe in ME. I am a capable*

*person. I can do it. I can handle anything
that comes my way. I believe in possibilities.*

4.   Anytime you see your reflection today,
     repeat these affirmations: *I am at peace. I
     have all the time I need. I flow with life easily
     and effortlessly.*

The Power Is Within You:
Your Day 17 Journaling Exercise

1.   Close your eyes and drift back to your
     past. See yourself when you were five
     years old. Where are you? At school? At
     home? What do you like to do? How do
     you view the world? Open your eyes and
     write down whatever comes to mind.

2.   Do you remember any of the worries or
     negative beliefs that you had when you
     were five years old? Do you remember any
     hurt feelings? Write them all down.

3.   Next to all the beliefs you wrote down
     in Step 2, write down the real reasons
     for these beliefs. Perhaps your parents
     were having a bad day at work and told

you something that wasn't true. Perhaps a childhood friend who was unloved decided to take it out on you. Write all your thoughts in your journal.

4. Make a list of some of the things that are causing you stress this week. Do any of them have to do with the limited thinking of your five-year-old consciousness? Take time to write down your innermost thoughts and reflections.

Your Heart Thought for Day 17: *I Experience the Totality of Possibilities Within Me*

What does *the totality of possibilities* mean to you? Think of it as going beyond all limitations. Let your mind go beyond thoughts like *It can't be done. It won't work. There's not enough time. There are too many obstacles.*

Think of how often you have expressed these limitations: *Because I'm a woman, I can't do this. Because I'm a man, I can't do that. I don't have what it takes.* You hold on to limitations because they are important to you. But limitations stop you from expressing and experiencing the totality of possibilities. Every time you think *I can't*, you are limiting yourself. Are you willing to go beyond what you believe today?

Your Day 17 Meditation:
Affirmations for a Stress-free Life
(Day 17 of the audio download)

Negative, fearful thinking only brings more stress into your life. Here are some affirmations you can say wherever you are—in front of your mirror, in the car, at your desk—when negative thoughts begin to surface:

I let go of all fear and doubt, and life becomes simple and easy for me.

I create a stress-free world for myself.

I breathe in and out slowly, relaxing more and more with each breath.

I am a capable person, and I can handle anything that comes my way.

I am centered and focused, and I feel more secure with each day.

It is safe to express how I feel.

I can remain serene in any situation.

I trust myself to deal with any problems that arise during the day.

I realize that stress is only fear. I now release all fears.

DAY 18

Receiving Your Prosperity

Are you a magnet for miracles, money, prosperity, and abundance? Today you learn how you can be when you open yourself to receiving.

This is a good time to go back and look at the notes you wrote in your journal when you first started this course. Do you see how much you have learned? Can you see how much more comfortable you are with saying your affirmations in front of the mirror? You are a magnet for miracles!

Do you believe that you are also a magnet for money, prosperity, and abundance? There is so much abundance in the world just waiting for you to experience it. There is more money than you could ever spend. There is more joy than you could ever imagine. There are more people than you could ever meet. If you fully understood this, you would realize that you can have everything you need and desire.

mirror work

The Power within us is willing to give us our fondest dreams and enormous abundance in an instant. Are you open to receiving it? If you want something, the Universe doesn't say, "I'll think about it." It readily responds and sends it through. However, you must be open and ready in order to receive it.

I have noticed that sometimes when people come to my lectures, they sit with their arms folded across their chests. How are they going to let anything in? It is a wonderful gesture to open your arms wide so that the Universe notices and responds.

I invite you to do that right now. Stand up, open your arms, and say, *I am open and receptive to all the good and abundance in the Universe.* Now shout it from the rooftops for everyone to hear!

Prosperity can mean many things—money, love, success, comfort, beauty, time, knowledge. You create prosperity by talking and thinking about your abundance. You cannot create prosperity by talking or thinking about your lack. When you concentrate on lack, it only creates more lack. Poverty thinking brings more poverty. Gratitude thinking brings more abundance.

Your mirror work is a very powerful tool that will help bring more prosperity into your life. When you allow the abundance of the Universe to flow through your experiences, you can receive everything you desire. All it takes is practice and your mirror!

Whatever you give out comes back to you. Always. If you take from life, then life will take from you. It's that simple. You may feel that you do not steal, but are you counting the paper clips and stamps you are taking home from the office? Are you a person who steals time or robs others of respect? All these things are telling the Universe, "I don't really deserve the good in life. I have to sneak it, steal it."

Be aware of the beliefs that may be blocking the flow of money and prosperity in your life. Then use your mirror work to change those beliefs and create new, abundant thinking. The best thing you can do if you are having money problems is to develop prosperity thinking.

There are two prosperity affirmations I have used for many years that work well for me. They will work for you, too. They are: *My income is constantly increasing* and *I prosper wherever I turn.*

When something good comes into your life, say *Yes!* to it. Open yourself to receiving good. Say *Yes!* to your world. Opportunities and prosperity will increase a hundredfold. Once a day, stand with your arms open wide and say with joy: *I am open and receptive to all the abundance in the Universe. Thank you, life*. Life will hear you and respond.

Let's affirm: *Life supplies all my needs in great abundance. I trust life.*

Your Day 18 Mirror Work Exercise

1. Today your mirror work is going to focus on receiving your prosperity. Stand up with your arms outstretched and say: *I am open and receptive to all good.*

2. Now look into the mirror and say it again: *I am open and receptive to all good.* Let the words flow from your heart: *I am open and receptive to all good.*

3. Repeat this affirmation ten more times.

4. Notice how you feel. Do you feel liberated? Do this exercise every morning until the end of your mirror work course. It's a wonderful way to increase your prosperity consciousness.

The Power Is Within You:
Your Day 18 Journaling Exercise

1. What are your beliefs about money? Go back to the mirror. Look into your eyes and say: *My biggest fear about money is [fill in your fear].* Write down your answer and why you feel this way.

2. What did you learn about money as a child? How were finances handled in your family? How do you handle money now? Write your thoughts down. Do you see any patterns?

3. Now do some journaling to shift yourself into prosperity thinking. Write down what it would be like to have all the things you have always wanted. What would they be? What would your life look like then? Where would you travel? What would you do? Feel it. Enjoy it. Be creative and *have fun.*

Your Heart Thought for Day 18:
I Am a Yes Person

I know that I am one with all life. I am surrounded by and permeated with Infinite Wisdom. Therefore, I rely totally on the Universe to support me in every positive way. Everything I could possibly need is already here waiting for me. This planet has more food on it than I could possibly eat. There is more money than I could ever spend. There are more people than I could ever meet. There is more love than I could possibly experience. There is more joy than I can even imagine. This world has everything I need and desire. It is all mine to use and to have.

The One Infinite Mind, the One Infinite Intelligence, always says *yes* to me. No matter what I choose to believe or think or say, the Universe always says *yes*. I do not waste my time on negative thinking or negative subjects. I choose to see myself and life in the most positive ways.

I say *Yes!* to opportunity and prosperity. I say *Yes!* to all good. I am a *Yes!* person living in a *Yes!* world, being responded to by a *Yes!* Universe, and I rejoice that this is so.

I am grateful to be one with Universal Wisdom and backed by Universal Power.

Your Day 18 Meditation: Receiving Prosperity
(Day 18 of the audio download)

You can never create prosperity by talking about or thinking about your lack of money. This is wasted thinking and cannot bring you abundance. Dwelling on lack only creates more lack. Poverty thinking brings more poverty. Gratitude thinking brings abundance.

There are a few attitudes and affirmations that are guaranteed to keep prosperity beyond reach. Resenting other people for the amount of money they have just puts up a wall between you and your own flow. And negative affirmations like *There is never enough money* and *Money goes out faster than it comes in* represent poverty thinking of the worse kind. The Universe can respond only to what you believe about yourself and about life. Examine whatever negative thoughts you have about money and then decide to let them go. They have not served you well in the past, and they will not serve you well in the future.

You can buy an occasional lottery ticket for fun, but do not put a lot of attention into winning the lottery and thinking that will solve your problems. This is scarcity thinking and will not create lasting good. Winning the lottery seldom brings positive changes in anyone's life. In fact, most lottery winners lose almost all their winnings within the first two years and are often worse off financially than before they won. If you think that winning the lottery will solve all your problems, you are greatly mistaken, because it doesn't involve changing your consciousness. In effect, you're saying to the Universe, *I don't deserve to have good in my life except by a fluke.* If you change your thinking to allow the abundance of the Universe to flow through your experience, you can have all the things you think the lottery can bring you. And you will be able to keep them, because they will be yours by right of consciousness.

Affirming, declaring, deserving, and *allowing* are the steps to attracting riches far greater than you could ever win in a lottery. Open your consciousness to new ideas about money, and it will be yours.

If you want to bring more money and prosperity into your life, repeat these affirmations with feeling:

> *I am a magnet for money. Prosperity of every kind is drawn to me.*
> *At work, I am deeply appreciated and well compensated.*
> *I live in a loving, abundant, harmonious universe, and I am grateful.*
> *I am open to the unlimited prosperity that exists everywhere.*

The law of attraction brings only good into my life. I move from poverty thinking to prosperity thinking, and my finances reflect this change.

Good comes to me from everywhere and everyone.

I express gratitude for all the good in my life. Each day brings wonderful new surprises.

I pay my bills with love, and I rejoice as I write out each check. Abundance flows freely through me.

I deserve the best, and I accept the best now.

I release all resistance to money and allow it to flow joyously into my life. My good comes from everywhere and everyone.

Living Your Attitude of Gratitude

*Today is devoted to thanking life for
all its many gifts and learning how to live
with an attitude of gratitude every day.*

Did you know that prosperity and gratitude go hand in hand? I am always grateful to be one with Universal Wisdom and backed by Universal Power. I have noticed that the Universe loves gratitude. The more grateful you are, the more goodies you get. When I say *goodies*, I don't mean only material things. I mean all the people, places, and experiences that make life so wonderfully worth living.

You know how great you feel when your life is filled with love and joy and health and creativity, and you get green lights and parking places? This is how our lives are meant to be lived. This is how our lives can be if we are grateful. The Universe is a generous, abundant giver, and it likes to be appreciated.

Think about how you feel when you give a friend a present. If the person looks at it and frowns or says, "It's not my style" or "I'd never use anything like that," then you will have little desire to ever give that person a present again. However, if your friend's eyes dance with delight, and she is pleased and thankful, then every time you see something she would like, you will want to give it to her.

For quite some time now, I have been accepting every compliment and every present with the thought: *I accept this with joy and pleasure and gratitude.* I have learned that the Universe loves this expression, and I constantly get the most wonderful presents!

Be grateful from the moment you wake up in the morning. If you start the day by saying, "Thank you, bed, for a good night's sleep," from this beginning it is easy to think of many, many more things to be grateful for. By the time I have gotten out of bed, I have probably expressed gratitude for 80 or 100 different people, places, things, and experiences in my life.

In the evening, just before you go to sleep, review your day and bless and be grateful for all your experiences— even the challenging ones. If you feel that you made a mistake or made a decision that was not the best, forgive yourself.

Be grateful for all the lessons you have learned, even the painful ones. They are little treasures that have been given to you. As you learn from them, your life will change for the better. Rejoice when you see a portion of the dark side of yourself. This means that you are ready to let go of something that has been hindering you. At that moment, you can say: *Thank you for showing me this, so I can heal it and move on.*

Spend as many moments as you can today and every day being grateful for all the good in your life. If you have little good in your life now, it will increase. If you have an abundant life now, it will increase. This is a win-win situation. You are happy, and the Universe is happy. This attitude of gratitude increases your abundance.

When you interact with people today, tell them how grateful you are for what they've done. Tell sales clerks, waiters, postal workers, employers, employees, friends, family, and perfect strangers. Let's help make this a world of grateful and thankful giving and receiving!

Let's affirm: *I joyously give to life, and life lovingly gives back to me.*

Your Day 19 Mirror Work Exercise

1. When you first wake up in the morning and open your eyes, say these affirmations to yourself: *Good morning, bed. I am so grateful for the warmth and comfort you have given me. Darling [Name], this is a blessed day. All is well.*

2. Take a few more minutes to relax in your bed and think of all the things you are grateful for.

3. When you're ready to get up, go to the bathroom mirror. Look sweetly and deeply into your eyes. List the many things you are grateful for. Say them as affirmations: *I am grateful for my beautiful smile. I am grateful to feel perfectly healthy today. I am grateful for having a job to go to today. I am grateful for the friends I am going to meet today.*

4. Whenever you pass a mirror today, stop and say an affirmation for something you are grateful for in that moment.

The Power Is Within You:
Your Day 19 Journaling Exercise

1. Feed your attitude of gratitude every day: start a gratitude journal. Write down at least one thing that you are grateful for. Write down everything you are grateful for. Write an affirmation for each thing you are grateful for, to use in your mirror work.

2. Read inspiring stories about the power of gratitude. (My book *Gratitude: A Way of Life* contains contributions from 48 of the most inspiring people I know, and you can also find stories in *An Attitude of Gratitude: 21 Life Lessons* by Keith D. Harrell.) Write down an inspiring story of gratitude from your own experience or from the life of someone you know.

Your Heart Thought for Day 19:
I Give and Receive Gifts Graciously

Deep at the center of my being, there is an infinite well of gratitude. I now allow this gratitude to fill my heart, my body, my mind, my consciousness, my very being. This gratitude radiates out from me in all directions, touching everything in my world, and returns to me as more to be grateful for. The more gratitude I feel, the more aware I am that the supply is endless.

Appreciation and acceptance act like powerful magnets for miracles every moment of the day. Compliments are gifts of prosperity. I have learned to accept them graciously. If somebody compliments me, I smile and say, "Thank you."

Today is a sacred gift from life. I open my arms wide to receive the full measure of prosperity that the Universe offers. Any time of the day or night, I can let it in.

The Universe supports me in every way possible. I live in a loving, abundant, harmonious Universe, and I am grateful. There are times in life, however, when the Universe gives to me but I am not in a position to do anything about giving back. I can think of many people who helped me enormously at times when there was no way I could ever repay them. Later, however, I was able to help others, and that's the way life goes. I relax and rejoice in the abundance and gratitude that are here now.

Your Day 19 Meditation: The Light Has Come
(Day 19 of the audio download)

This is an exercise for two people, so invite a friend or family member to join you.

Sit facing your partner. Hold each other's hands and look into each other's eyes. Take a nice, deep breath and release any fear you may have. Take another deep breath, release your judgment, and allow yourself just to be with this person.

What you see in your partner is a reflection of you, a reflection of what is in you. We are all one. We breathe the same air. We drink the same water. We eat the foods of the earth. We have the same desires and needs. We all want to be healthy. We all want to love and be loved. We all want to live comfortably and peacefully. And we want to prosper. We all want to live our lives with fulfillment.

Allow yourself to look at your partner with love, and be willing to receive the love back. Know that you are safe. Affirm perfect health for your partner. Affirm loving relationships so that your partner is surrounded by loving people at all times. Affirm prosperity so that your partner can live comfortably. Affirm comfort and safety for your partner. Knowing that what you give out returns to you multiplied, affirm the very best of everything for your partner. It is deserved. See your partner willing to accept it. And so it is.

DAY 20

Teaching Mirror
Work to Children

*Children also face the stresses of life. Today
you learn how to practice mirror work with little
ones, and you watch the miracles that happen.*

You are nearly at the end of this course and you
are doing beautifully. I applaud your commitment and
dedication! Every day you practice your mirror work,
you are giving yourself the gift of love. And every day
you practice your mirror work, you are letting go of
old, negative beliefs you have been carrying around
for so long. Where did these negative beliefs come
from? We picked them up as children. We absorbed
every word that was said to us. The more we heard our
parents or other adults saying negative things about
us, the more we believed them.

Growing up, we often called one another cruel and hurtful names and belittled one another. But why did we do this? Where did we learn such behavior? Many of us were told by our parents or teachers that we were stupid or dumb or lazy, that we were troublemakers or not good enough. Maybe we cringed when we heard these statements, but we believed them. Little did we realize how much these beliefs hurt, or how deeply embedded our pain and shame would become.

Look back at some of the more difficult lessons of this course, lessons in which you uncovered beliefs that were blocking you. When you did your mirror work and journaling, did you find that those beliefs often stemmed from past hurts from your childhood?

I was not taught in school that my choice of words would have an effect on my life. No one taught me that my thoughts were creative, that they could literally shape my destiny, or that what I gave out verbally would return to me as life experiences. No one ever taught me that I was worth loving or that I deserved to have good things happen to me. Certainly nobody taught me that life was here to support me.

We can change all that for our children now. One of the most important things we can do for them is to remind them of the basic truth that they are lovable.

Our role as parents is not to be perfect, to get everything right, but to be loving and kind.

Children today have a lot more issues to deal with than we did when we were their age. They are steadily barraged with news about the critical state of the world and are continually having to make complex choices. How children handle these challenges is a direct reflection of how they truly feel about themselves. The more children love and respect themselves, the easier it will be for them to make the right choices in life.

It is important that we instill in our children a sense of independence and power and the knowledge that they can make a difference in today's world. Above all, it is important to teach them to love who they are and to know that they are good enough no matter what.

Young people are looking up to us and listening to every word we say. Be a shining example of positive statements and affirmations. When you begin to believe them, so will your children.

Nurture the children in your life just as you are learning to nurture yourself. Remember: nobody has the "perfect" child or the "perfect" parent. We are bound to make poor choices at one time or another. That is simply part of the learning and growing

process. What is important is to love your child unconditionally and, most important, to love *yourself* unconditionally. Then watch the miracles happen for your
children as well as for yourself.

Let's affirm: *I can be what I want to be. I can do what
I want to do. All life supports me.*

Your Day 20 Mirror Work Exercise

1. I would like you to watch a video of a
   sweet little girl doing her affirmations.
   It's called "Jessica's 'Daily Affirmation,'"
   and you can see it at **www.youtube.com/
   watch?v=qR3rK0kZFkg**.

2. Watch this video with your child or any
   child in your life, even with your inner
   child.

3. Ask your child to do its own daily
   affirmations just as Jessica did in the
   video. Ask the child what it is happy
   about and have it tell that to the mirror.

4. You can start this exercise by doing your
   own mirror work and inviting your child
   to join in. Say simple affirmations like: *I*

love you. I love everything about you. I am
great! I am beautiful! I have cool hair! I can
dance like a TV star!

5. Schedule a time every day to do mirror
    work with your child, even if only for a
    few minutes in the morning.

The Power Is Within You:
Your Day 20 Journaling Exercise

1. Begin today's journaling exercise by
    reading a story excerpted from my book
    The Adventures of Lulu. You can access
    it by visiting **www.louisehay.com/
    learning-mirror-work.**

2. Have drawing paper, colored pencils,
    colored markers, crayons, and glue ready,
    and ask your child to draw a Magic Mirror
    to go to, just as Lulu does in the book.
    Encourage the child to decorate the
    mirror: glue pretty pictures around it, add
    glitter and sparkles to the frame, cover it
    in a riot of color.

3. With your child, take turns looking in the Magic Mirror and saying wonderful things about yourself.

4. Write down the positive statements you and your child say, so you can repeat them when you do your morning mirror work together.

Your Heart Thought for Day 20:
I Communicate Openly with My Children

It is vitally important to keep the lines of communication open with children, especially during the teen years. So often children are told things like *Don't say that. Don't do that. Don't feel that. Don't be that way. Don't express that.* When all they hear is *don't, don't, don't,* they stop communicating.

Then, when the children are older, parents complain, "My children never call me." Why don't they call? Because the lines of communication have been cut, that's why.

When you are open with your children—using positive statements like "It's okay to feel sad" and "You can talk to me about it"—and you encourage them to share their feelings, the lines of communication will be restored.

Your Day 20 Meditation: Welcome the Child
(Day 20 of the audio download)

Place a hand over your heart. Close your eyes. Allow yourself not only to *see* your inner child but also to *be* that child. Ask someone to read the following paragraph to you. Imagine you are hearing your parents tell you:

> *We're so glad you came. We've been waiting for you. We wanted you so much to be part of our family. You're so important to us. The family wouldn't be the same without you. We love you. We want to hold you. We want to help you grow up to be all that you can be. You don't have to be like us. You can be yourself. We love your uniqueness. You're so beautiful. You're so bright. You're so creative. It gives us such pleasure to have you here. We thank you for choosing our family. We know you're blessed. You have blessed us by coming. We love you. We really love you.*

Let your little child make these words true for you. Be aware that every day you can look in the mirror and say these words. You can tell yourself all the things you wanted your parents to tell you. Your little child needs to feel wanted and loved. Give that to your child.

No matter how old you are or how sick or scared the little child within you is, it needs to be wanted and loved. Keep telling your inner child, "I want you, and I love you." It is the truth for you. The Universe wants you here. And that's why you are here. You've always been loved and will always be loved throughout eternity. You can live happily ever after. And so it is.

DAY 21

Loving Yourself Now

Through mirror work, you discover that
you are perfect just as you are and that loving
yourself can heal every problem.

Congratulations, dear ones! This is the last day of your 21-day adventure in mirror work. It has brought you closer to discovering one of the biggest treasures of your life—the gift of loving yourself.

This was not an easy journey, I know. There were a few bumps and stumbling blocks along the way, but you stuck with it. I am so very proud of you!

Throughout this journey, you have used your mirror work to help you examine your self-talk, quiet your inner critic, forgive those who have hurt you, let go of past fears, and release old beliefs and negative thought patterns. In doing so, you have opened a storehouse of treasure within you.

My wish for you is to always remember that there is one thing that heals every problem, and that is to *love yourself.* When you start to love yourself more each day, it's amazing how your life will get better. You will feel better. You will get the job you want. You will have the money you need. Your relationships will improve, and the negative ones will dissolve and new ones will appear.

Although you have completed this course, your mirror work has only just begun. It is something for you to practice every day. You will most likely encounter more bumps and even a few detours as you continue the journey. But you will be ready. You will be able to pick yourself up, look into your mirror, and remind yourself that you are worth loving. You are perfect just as you are. You deserve all the goodies in life. You are a magnet for miracles.

Carry your mirror with you. Keep reminding the beautiful person looking back at you that you love this person with all your heart.

Let's affirm: *When I express love toward myself and everyone I meet, that love comes right back to me!*

In my Afterword (page 181), I will leave you with a list of 12 ways you can love yourself now. Let them serve as reminders of the good work you have done over the past three weeks. And remember: I love you!

Your Day 21 Mirror Play Exercise

1. Go to the mirror and look at the beautiful person looking back at you. Raise your arms and give yourself a big cheer for finishing this course. Say these affirmations: *I love you, darling. I really love you. You did it! You completed this course. I am so proud of you. You can do anything you set your mind to.*

2. Take time to express your gratitude for all the work you have done. Say these affirmations: *Thank you for hanging in there. Thank you for being open to learning something new. I really love you.*

3. Make a commitment to continue your mirror play. Say: *I will see you tomorrow, gorgeous. We will discuss other areas that I'd like to change. I love you. You are worth loving. You deserve only the best.*

The Power Is Within You:
Your Day 21 Journaling Exercise

1. Review your journal from the beginning of the course. Go through each lesson and congratulate yourself for all the work you have done.

2. Write down the areas where you have progressed the most. Write down some of the problems areas where you could use more work.

3. Go back and repeat the lessons in which you feel you need more guidance from your mirror.

4. If you like, share your comments about this course on my Facebook page, **www .facebook.com/louiselhay**.

5. Now go play with your inner child!

Your Heart Thought for Day 21:
We Are All Part of the Harmonious Whole

Remember: you are part of a community of people all over the globe who are working to make this a better world. We have come together at this time because there is something we need to learn from one another. It is safe for us to work on loving ourselves so that we may benefit and grow from this experience. We choose to work together to create harmony in our relationships and in every area of our lives.

Divine right action is guiding us every moment of the day. We say the right words at the right time and follow the right course of action at all times. Each person is part of the harmonious whole.

There is a divine blending of energies as we work joyfully together, supporting and encouraging one another in ways that are fulfilling and productive. We are healthy, happy, loving, joyful, respectful, supportive, and at peace with ourselves and with one another. So be it, and so it is.

Your Day 21 Meditation: A World That Is Safe
(Day 21 of the audio download)

We've touched on many things in the past 21 days. We've talked about negative things and positive things. We've talked about fears and frustrations. Many of us still do not trust ourselves to take care of ourselves, and we feel lost and lonely. Yet we have been working on ourselves for some time and have noticed that our lives are changing. Lots of problems in the past aren't problems anymore. It doesn't change overnight, but if we are persistent and consistent, positive things *do* happen. So let's share the energy we have, and the love we have, with other people. Know that as we give from our hearts we are also receiving from other hearts.

Let's open our hearts so that we can take in everyone with love, support, and caring. Let's move that love to people in the street who have no homes and no place to go. Let's share our love with those who are angry, frightened, or in pain. Let's send love to the people who are in the process of leaving the planet and those who have already left.

Let's share our love with everybody, whether they accept it or not. Let's hold the entire planet in our hearts: the animals, the vegetation, and all the people. The people we are angry at or frustrated with. Those who are not doing things our way. And those who are expressing so-called evil—let's take them into our hearts, too, so that from a feeling of safety they can begin to recognize who they really are.

See peace breaking out all over the planet. Know that you are contributing to that peace right now. Rejoice that you have the ability to do something positive to help. Acknowledge how wonderful you are. Know that it is the truth for you. And so it is.

AFTERWORD

I am so happy, dear reader, to have been able to share with you the practice of mirror work, which has been so valuable to me in my life. My hope is that you, too, will find mirror work valuable as a vehicle for positive growth and self-care.

In closing, I would like to leave you with 12 ways you can love yourself now—and always. Let them serve as reminders of what you have learned over the past three weeks and provide you with ongoing support for a joyous and fulfilling life.

And always remember: I love you!

Louise Hay

12 Ways You Can Love Yourself Now—and Always

1. **Stop All Criticism.**
   Criticism never changes a thing. Refuse to criticize yourself. Accept yourself exactly as you are. Everybody changes. When you criticize yourself, your changes are negative. When you approve of yourself, your changes are positive.

2. **Forgive Yourself.**
   Let the past go. You did the best you could at the time, with the understanding, awareness, and knowledge that you had. Now you are growing and changing, and you will live life differently.

3. **Don't Scare Yourself.**
   Stop terrorizing yourself with your thoughts. It's a dreadful way to live. Find a mental image that gives you pleasure and immediately switch a scary thought to a pleasant thought.

4. **Be Gentle and Kind and Patient.**
    Be gentle with yourself. Be kind to yourself.
    Be patient with yourself as you learn new
    ways of thinking. Treat yourself as you would
    treat anyone you really love.

5. **Be Kind to Your Mind.**
    Self-hatred is hating your own thoughts.
    Don't hate yourself for *having* the thoughts.
    Gently change the thoughts to more life-
    affirming ones.

6. **Praise Yourself.**
    Criticism breaks down your inner spirit.
    Praise builds it up. Praise yourself as much as
    you can. Tell yourself how well you are doing
    with every little thing.

7. **Support Yourself.**
    Find ways to support yourself. Reach out
    to friends and allow them to help you. It is
    being strong to ask for help when you need it.

8. **Be Loving to Your Negatives.**
    Acknowledge that you created them to fulfill
    a need. Now you are finding new, positive
    ways to fulfill those needs. Lovingly release
    the old, negative patterns.

9. **Take Care of Your Body.**
   Learn about nutrition. What kind of fuel does your body need in order to have optimum energy and vitality? Learn about exercise. What kind of exercise do you enjoy? Cherish and revere the temple you live in.

10. **Have Fun!**
    Remember the things that gave you joy as a child and incorporate them into your life now. Find a way to have fun with everything you do. Let yourself express the joy of living. Smile. Laugh. Rejoice, and the Universe rejoices with you!

11. **Love Yourself . . . Do It Now.**
    Don't wait until you get well or lose weight or get a new job or find a new relationship. Begin loving yourself now—and do the best you can.

12. **Do Your Mirror Work.**
    Look into your eyes often. Express the growing sense of love you have for yourself. Forgive yourself while looking into the mirror. Talk to your parents while looking into the mirror. Forgive them, too. At least once.

ABOUT THE AUTHOR

Louise Hay was an inspirational teacher who educated millions since the 1984 publication of her bestseller *You Can Heal Your Life*, which has more than 50 million copies in print worldwide. Renowned for demonstrating the power of affirmations to bring about positive change, Louise was the author of more than 30 books for adults and children, including the bestsellers *The Power Is Within You* and *Heal Your Body*. In addition to her books, Louise produced numerous audio and video programs, card decks, online courses, and other resources for leading a healthy, joyous, and fulfilling life.

Websites: www.louisehay.com, www.healyourlife .com, and www.facebook.com/louiselhay

Hay House Titles of Related Interest

YOU CAN HEAL YOUR LIFE, the movie,
starring Louise Hay & Friends
(available as an online streaming video)
www.hayhouse.com/louise-movie

THE SHIFT, the movie,
starring Dr. Wayne W. Dyer
(available as an online streaming video)
www.hayhouse.com/the-shift-movie

THE ANSWER IS SIMPLE . . . LOVE YOURSELF,
LIVE YOUR SPIRIT!, by Sonia Choquette

I CAN SEE CLEARLY NOW, by Dr. Wayne W. Dyer

LIFE LOVES YOU: 7 Spiritual Practices to Heal Your Life,
by Louise Hay and Robert Holden

MIRACLES NOW: 108 Life-Changing Tools for Less Stress, More
Flow, and Finding Your True Purpose, by Gabrielle Bernstein

YOU CAN CREATE AN EXCEPTIONAL LIFE,
by Louise Hay and Cheryl Richardson

All of the above are available at your local bookstore,
or may be ordered by contacting Hay House (see following page).

We hope you enjoyed this Hay House book. If you'd like to receive our online catalog featuring additional information on Hay House books and products, or if you'd like to find out more about the Hay Foundation, please contact:

Hay House, Inc., P.O. Box 5100, Carlsbad, CA 92018-5100
(760) 431-7695 or (800) 654-5126
(760) 431-6948 (fax) or (800) 650-5115 (fax)
www.hayhouse.com® • www.hayfoundation.org

———

Published in Australia by: Hay House Australia Pty. Ltd.,
18/36 Ralph St., Alexandria NSW 2015
Phone: 612-9669-4299 • *Fax:* 612-9669-4144
www.hayhouse.com.au

Published in the United Kingdom by: Hay House UK, Ltd.,
The Sixth Floor, Watson House, 54 Baker Street, London W1U 7BU
Phone: +44 (0)20 3927 7290 • *Fax:* +44 (0)20 3927 7291
www.hayhouse.co.uk

Published in India by: Hay House Publishers India,
Muskaan Complex, Plot No. 3, B-2, Vasant Kunj, New Delhi 110 070
Phone: 91-11-4176-1620 • *Fax:* 91-11-4176-1630
www.hayhouse.co.in

———

Access New Knowledge.
Anytime. Anywhere.

Learn and evolve at your own pace
with the world's leading experts.

www.hayhouseU.com

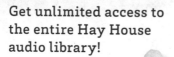